MOMT HER I LOVE YOU:

an adopting family's journey toward wholeness

Veronica Brunner

For Cheri
10-71-01
Ann

WovenWord Press

For information write:
WovenWord Press
811 Mapleton Avenue
Boulder, Colorado 80304

Cover and book design © 2001 by Vicki McVey

ISBN: 0967842824

Library of Congress Control Number: 2001089489
Family/Adoption/Psychology/Spirituality

Momther I Love You:
An Adopting Family's Journey Toward Wholeness
Veronica Brunner

Table of Contents

This book is dedicated, in hope and determination,
to all adoptive parents.

How Our Adoptive
Family Began

1

"Mom, I've decided to love you. I'm going to love this whole family," Cathie announced in a decisive tone as she emerged from a half-hour of silence in her room. I was at our dining room table, which is close to the long narrow kitchen. Her room was across the hall behind the kitchen. She walked to the far end of the kitchen to make her announcement. We were all there. At the age of eight she was freeing herself from her abusive and neglectful birth parents. It had been four years and three months since she had first walked through our front door as a foster child. My husband, Brian, and I had adopted Cathie and her biological brother, Tommy, along with a foster brother, Chris, two years earlier. Cathie had waited all this time for her birth parents to return; keeping herself distant, isolated, and starved for affection. Since they did not return, she had finally decided to accept our family as hers.

Brian quietly observed the burst of emotion and promise of love. "This I've got to see," he said as he continued to prepare one of his usual breakfasts of eggs, bacon, pancakes, and coffee. Tommy and Chris just looked at her and smiled. I assured Brian that I believed she knew what she was saying. It was such a surprise to hear her express these feelings. Cathie meant it. Her decision to love our family was a commitment that she took seriously. The next day she showed this by making a picture. First she printed: "MOMTHER, I LOVE YOU. YOU LOVE ME." Then she drew a clock and put the correct time on it. Under the clock was the date. I understood this to mean that she knew this was forever. It was definitely a big occasion, and one that will never be forgotten. She had thought about it a lot. As she handed the drawing to me, she said, "I know you will always love me. You will never leave me like my other mommy and daddy did." Now she waited for my affirmation.

"You are right. Daddy and I will never leave you," I assured her. I accepted the picture and quietly hugged her. WOW! What a giant leap this was for Cathie and our family. Now she wanted to be included in the family and in the hugging. No more standing aloof while Tommy and Chris came for hugs. I thanked God with all my heart.

Cathie's whole attitude changed. Her happy little face beamed everywhere we went. She was no longer negative. Temper tantrums that caused slamming doors, stomping up and down the stairs, or just throwing food or dishes decreased from eight or nine times a day to two or three a week. When asked to help, she was happy to please. Our whole family lightened up and began to blossom.

Friends asked us what happened to make such a difference. When I explained her decision to love us, they mirrored my sense of awe exactly—WOW!

We were now a family. It had seemed like such a long process for Brian and me, but we didn't mind the struggle now that we finally had what we both wanted most—our own family. It took faith, prayer, and confidence in God's plan for all of us. Brian was the youngest of fourteen children and I was the seventh in a family of thirteen. We were both raised with the same family values. Our parents believed that children were the greatest of all treasures. The fact that money was scarce helped us to care about each other rather than things. Nothing super-seded family. Our parents' joy and often only entertainment was their children. We were taught to have respect for each other, our church, and our country. We did.

My brother's aerial view of our family farm.

When I was just five years old, my much loved and deeply religious mother told me one night after family rosary that it was God's will for me to become a member of a religious group known as "Sisters." I remember feeling both disappointed and honored. On the one hand I loved my dolls and wanted to have a family like Mom. On the other hand it seemed so special for God to want me to be like my mother's three sisters, who were all members of the religious community that my mother was con-vinced I had been born to join. She told me that I had been her smallest baby and she didn't think I could ever have children. She had me baptized the day after my birth just in case I was too sickly to live. For my name she chose the name of the foundress of the religious community her sisters had joined. I knew that they were held in high esteem by all of my relatives. It would mean that I would belong to an elite group of holy people.

So, thinking that I had no choice of my own, I prayed as my mother told me to become a good sister some day. At fourteen I went to the convent and stayed nearly twenty years. At thirty-three I finally heard a superior say the words I had been waiting to hear all those years: "Sister, you are so unhappy. Why don't you leave?" We had been instructed at the convent that unless we heard this suggestion from a superior, we could not leave without endangering our eternal life of happiness. In other words, we could go to hell if we left the convent just because we chose to leave. I said to my superior, "I've waited all these years to hear someone give me permission to leave. Now, I've been here so long, I don't know how to handle leaving."

She was so wonderful, I couldn't believe it was true. She told me she knew a good priest with a degree in psychology who could help me. She set up the first appointment for me. Now I was free to do what I wanted instead of what my mother wanted. I just hoped it wasn't too late to have a family.

Most of my brothers and sisters already had families and were well aware of my unhappiness in the convent; when I told them I was leaving, they were all very supportive. They wanted me to be happy, that was all. I was afraid they would be disappointed with my lack of resolve, so it helped me very much to start communicating with them. My sweet mother apologized over and over again for telling me what to do with my life. For a while I was resentful, but after I gave it some thought, I realized she was doing what she thought was right at the time. Once I forgave her, I was free to go on with my dreams.

My years in the convent were not wasted by any means. They helped prepare me for the huge task God knew was waiting for me. The first six years of convent life were well spent in practicing self-discipline and prayer, and learning to get along with hundreds of other sisters. Tolerance was a necessity. Then, for fourteen years I was a teacher, dedicated to helping children learn and expand their minds. I spent much of my free time dreaming wistfully about raising my own family, and later discovered that this long wait for a family helped me in important ways. It helped me be patient and understanding, and taught me to keep my priorities straight in times of turmoil. Little problems were just that: little problems.

When I left my religious community I felt like a teenager free from parental control for the first time. I had a tremendous amount to learn about independent living, but everything was so exciting to me that I found myself in a state of euphoria most of the time. One of my sisters and brothers-in-law, thirteen hundred miles away, invited me to stay with their family until I found my own place and a job. I was very grateful, and their family was wonderful to me. I was able to get a job teaching at a private school about thirty miles from their home, and I went at this job of teaching primary children with gusto and dedication. Of course, the parents were delighted.

After three years of teaching, I was encouraged by the family of one of my students to become a private tutor of religion. This I did and loved. I taught family religion classes for one hour a week for twenty-two families. We had wonderful group celebrations of Passover and first communions. We all enjoyed the community feeling at these classes and services.

Brian had a very different preparation for the life we were about to share. After four years in the navy, he found himself taking care of his aging parents. He was a steady, good worker at the local public utility plant, helping to produce electricity. After his father died peacefully in his sleep, he cared for his mother for several more years until she needed constant care in a nursing home. Then he began to wonder if he was ever going to have his own family. Being a shy homebody, he was not likely to easily meet a partner. His social life consisted mostly of family gatherings, fishing, and vacationing with a best buddy once in a while.

Brian's family's home on a beet farm.

Both of us were praying to meet good partners. I had already made the mistake of one very short bad marriage, which was annulled by my church. This made me more careful

about my choice of men. I now knew that I would need a partner who had been raised with the same family values I had
been. Our prayers were answered when I was inspired to call
the local senior center to ask if anyone knew a senior woman in
need of a live-in companion.

Sometimes things happen that go beyond coincidence. I will
always believe that someone in heaven placed me in a house
right across the street from Brian, where an eighty-eight year old
woman, looking for someone like me, had called the senior center the same day I did. I believe that a very dear young man,
who died of cystic fibrosis shortly before I found this place, is the
saint in heaven who helped me. He knew my hopes and dreams.

For three months I worked and dated several different men.
After a couple of heart breaks, the lovely senior lady I was helping gave me her opinion: "None of the men you have been seeing are worthy of you. The one you ought to be dating is right
over there." She pointed across the street to a man in his back
yard hanging out his laundry. He was not very romantic looking. He never seemed to do anything except go to work and
visit with a lady who came once in a while. So I asked her why
she thought he would be so good for me. She said that he was
unusually good to his mother, and relayed a story his mother
had told her: One day she had called him at work and cried
because she was so lonely. He told her not to feel lonely because
God was always with her. Wow! This just might be Mr. Right
for me. I took a second look across the street. He lived in a simple house with a plain lawn, nothing fancy. He was always
working and smiling. Could the man of my dreams be this
close? How could I meet him?

Since shyness is not one of my problems, I chose to take
the practical approach: I would ask him for help. My church

8

supported the relocation of Vietnamese families, and I had volunteered to purchase some used furniture for them. I needed a truck to get it to their apartment—Brian had a truck. So one day, when I saw him outside with the lady who visited him, I went across the street, introduced myself, and asked if he could give me some assistance with the furniture project. The lady introduced herself as his sister and him as Brian. I sensed that he was too shy to say very much, but he wanted to meet me. He was happy to help. Once the job was complete he went on with his life as if nothing had happened.

Challenges get my creative juices flowing, and I often encourage that process by reading self-help books. At that time my book of choice was *Your Erroneous Zones*, by Dr. Wayne W. Dyer. He explained that sometimes we allow ourselves to be frustrated unnecessarily by ridiculous societal mores. I realized this was exactly what I was doing by waiting for Brian to call me. I could just as easily call him, so I did. When I asked if he were interested in dating, he answered, "Yes, yes, yes!"

We decided our first date would be to go fishing at a nearby lake, where he and one of his sisters and brothers-in-law were members. As it turned out, I felt so comfortable with him it almost scared me. His family was so similar to mine that I immediately felt at home with them, and although I was thirteen hundred miles from my own home, it no longer seemed like it. And so, after seven months of fishing, eating out, going to movies, and hiking, we agreed that we were much happier now than we had ever been. We got married. The community of families and Bible Study groups that I taught put on our wedding, and it took place in the very same backyard where my friend with cystic fibrosis had lived, died, and had his funeral. It all felt so right that I knew my friend in heaven had inspired us. I was at peace and very grateful!

Brian and I had a honeymoon of fishing and hiking in the mountains, and then we returned to the excitement of buying our own home. We chose a brick ranch style with a cool basement for quiet sleeping when Brian had to work the third shift at his plant. We were very excited to have our own home and life together. We purchased furniture and trimmed our hedges and landscaped with enthusiasm. What happiness!

Everything was going well—maybe we would be able to have children, even though I was forty and Brian was forty-five.

Our second anniversary trip up Pike's Peak.

A year later, after a D and C, our doctor informed us that I would need surgery and even then I might not be able to conceive and carry a child. I remembered my mother telling me that she didn't think I would live through childbirth, and decided God had different plans for me. Brian agreed that he would rather adopt than take a chance on surgery. Besides, if God chose for me to get pregnant, I would. It was up to God now. We were at peace.

My Sources of Strength and Courage

My purposes in writing this book are to encourage other parents to never give up their dreams of having a family, and to help needy children get a chance at life. I am therefore going to include, at the end of each chapter, some of the sources I drew upon for the spiritual strength to keep going. In addition I will list some favorite book, music, and website resources, as well as some tips of my own for adoptive parents.

The first resource I would like to mention is my family—particularly my parents. They gave me the gifts of basic inner courage and tenacity. My mother's example of always putting God first showed her deep faith. When I was a child, my mother's family would come to visit about once a month. They talked energetically about what was going on in the world concerning God and the Church. My father did not enter into these conversations. He seemed uninterested, but I noticed that as a matter of personal character he never gave up on himself or us, no matter what. He was a strong authoritarian figure in my life. When I saw the movie The Ten Commandments, and heard the Egyptian pharaoh say, "So let it be written, so let it be done," I thought of my father. The sense of absolute unquestioning authority was the same.

After leaving the convent, in my need to integrate the two principles of having faith in and not questioning God, I began a long search. I read many books, attended dozens of religious seminars, and audited dozens more theology classes at the University of Notre Dame, Indiana. None of them answered my quest, but they all helped me become aware of the diversity of religious faiths, along with the common human need for God. As a child, I had always thought of God as a combination of my parents. When I prayed, I talked to God as if I were having a conversation with them. But this did not satisfy me. I felt an emptiness that left me lacking the peace I wanted so much. Then one day I saw an ad in the paper or church bulletin for a lecture on "peace" by a priest who had gone to India to study Eastern forms of meditation. I went and found the answer to my many years of searching. His lecture set my mind free from its narrow interpretation of scripture and philosophy of life.

I met with him after the lecture and asked if he had time to become my spiritual director. He did. We set up a weekly schedule for hiking in the nearby hills for one hour at a time. He taught me Zen meditation. I sat in a chair in my living room each day for twenty-five minutes with the simple task of repeating over and over: "I am Veronica. I am breathing." Then, in silence, I would feel old anxieties leave my consciousness.

I was physically exhausted from the relief of letting go of personal baggage, but it was summer break from school, so I could get extra sleep. For ten weeks before fall school began, I meditated, read scripture, rested, and went for weekly spiritual direction. By the time I made my yearly lesson plans for religion classes, I felt like a whole new person. When I shared the new insights with my student families they concurred with the refreshing consciousness I was experiencing: God was not limited to any one belief. We could all experience love and goodness everywhere just as we had learned as children.

I was now experiencing so much peace, and the families I taught so much joy, that I knew something my spiritual director told me was true: "The only real gift we can give someone is that of our own inner peace." It seemed clear to me that if I were to share peace with others I would need to meditate daily the rest of my life. I found that any day I skipped meditation I felt a lack of peace, and would be irritable and easily confused. I needed the daily centering, and found that with it I also experienced freedom from guilt. Previous to practicing Zen meditation I felt guilty for every small infraction, such as becoming impatient or having unkind thoughts. With this new thinking I learned that all actions have a particular karma or simple cause and effect. They are not necessarily bad or good. They just are. I learned to say "so what" to former problems, and to go on with life in peace. I could think more clearly and smile so much more easily. The joy and humor of life were evident to me. I became aware of God's presence everywhere. My mother had always been conscious of God coming first in life—now I owned this same faith. I felt well grounded. I can't emphasize too much the importance of Zen meditation in my life. At the same time, I can easily imagine that other forms of meditation may be equally valuable for other individuals. Joseph Campbell has told us that we each need to find our own bliss and go with it, and I have certainly found this to be true.

Tips For Adoptive Parents

✦ Wanting a family very much is the key to accepting problem children.

✦ Get as much preparation as possible to understand what it would be like to be an abandoned young child (see books by Dave Pelzer in the following section).

Books, Music, and Websites

⁓ Suzuki and Shunryu. *Zen Mind, Beginner's Mind*. New York: Weatherhill Publisher, 1970.

⁓ Campbell, Joseph and Bill Moyers. Printouts of a Public Affairs Television series: *The Hero's Adventure, The Message Of the Myth, The First Storytellers, Sacrifice and Bliss, Love and the Goddess, Masks Of Eternity*. Executive Producers: Joan Konner and Alvin H. Perlmutter. Aired 1988. Copies obtainable from Doubleday, P.O. Box 5071 DesPlaines, Illinois 60017.

⁓ Dyer, Dr. Wayne W. *Your Erroneous Zones*. New York: Avon, 1976. This book freed me from ridiculous social mores. It is a treasure for anyone suffering from excessive guilt and/or worries.

⁓ Pelzer, Dave. *A Child Called "It"*. Deerfield Beach, FL: Health Communications, Inc., 1995.

⁓ Pelzer, Dave.*The Lost Boy*. Deerfield Beach, FL: Health Communications, Inc., 1997.

⁓ Pelzer, Dave. *A Man Named Dave*. New York: Penguin, Putnam Inc., Plume Publisher, 1999.

❧ Foster Parent Associations Network—Community members share resources and search tips for those interested in foster parenting in the U.S.: http://www.fosterparents.com/states3/

❧ Foster Parents Resources—Join this network of foster parents for access to information, resources and support. Includes chat room and message board: http://fostercare.org/links/fplinks.htm

The County Agency

2

Since our ages were not conducive to long waiting, Brian and I wanted to get started with the adoption process as soon as possible. Both of us wanted younger children because we thought they would have fewer psychological problems. It seemed logical that smaller children would gradually absorb our own senses of morality and the family values we treasured.

We called our county Social Services agency, and inquired about adoption procedures. They warmly encouraged us to attend the next series of regularly scheduled adoptive parent conferences, where we met with four couples who were equally eager to form their own families. After we shared our hopes and dreams, the speaker warned us about expecting too much. Our children would have difficulty adjusting to us. It would be important, both for our own good and that of the children, to keep expectations low rather than high. All of us were encouraged to adopt older children because not many babies were available. We were somewhat disappointed, but we could accept this reality.

We were given four thick volumes of photographs of children in need of adoption. I felt so needed, but overwhelmed at the same time—so many children without families. Why? Where were their parents? How could they give up their children like that? I ignored my spinning head and began looking for a family for us. We thought two boys and two girls would be good, but there were so many of them! We selected a family that reminded us of our own when we were small. In the photo, the youngest child was fearfully clinging to the oldest. My heart went out to them—they needed us and we needed them. It seemed to us that they would fit into our extended families, so we asked for more information about them.

Then we had our first lesson in just how manipulative The System could be. We were told that since these children were from out of state, it was unlikely that we would be able to adopt them. What?! Then why show us their pictures and get us emotionally involved with the program?

We were told that when dealing with such needy children, any chance is better than no chance. If someone from out of state asked for a particular family, that caused the children in that family to be processed faster in their own state, helping them to be permanently placed—a matter of State Pride. Since the children would benefit from our asking for them, we did, but we never heard about them again.

Brian and I thought there just had to be a better way! We visited his cousins who were involved in the foster parent program in their county. We learned that foster children often become eligible for adoption after being with foster parents for several months or, sometimes, even years. This seemed to be a much better way of getting our family. We could get children quite young and establish family ties while they were in our foster care. This might even prevent the added trauma of transferring the children to a different adoptive home.

So we called Social Services back and asked to become a part of the county foster parent program. When we were cautioned not to expect to adopt the children put in our care, we knew they had read our minds—how funny! Once more we attended a required series of conferences. This was a much larger group of people who were lively and outspoken. And again, the speakers warned us to expect problems. Although this was emphasized over and over again, how could we ever imagine the reality? We were not told that once they were in our homes, the children would have a chance to tug at our heartstrings. They were pros at that, and they knew it—it was their strongest mechanism for self-preservation.

After the conferences we had a home study, which consisted of a social worker coming for a tour of our home and yard. She questioned us about our work habits and availability for children, and noticed that we were well located with respect to schools and medical facilities. It felt wonderful to be getting closer to having children in our home. Then she asked us, "Will you volunteer to take children who are in need of protective custody?" The question jolted us into the reality of what we were facing. Our foster children could be traumatized, unhappy, and uncooperative, but Brian and I believed completely in the absolute right of every child to have a chance. So, knowing we might be taking children with serious problems, we agreed to volunteer.

A month later we received our foster parent license in the mail. We were approved for as many as four children at a time. We had chosen the age range from birth to eight years. We were satisfied that this was going much better than the adoption program.

Throughout all of these preparations Brian was his usual quiet self. I did most of the talking. Due to his shy nature this was true everywhere we went. He was therefore questioned over and over as to what he thought about all of this. We laughed about this questioning. Of course he agreed to it, or he wouldn't have been there, and neither would I. As a matter of fact, most of the men at these conferences were quiet.

Our county Social Services agency invited us back for brief meetings during which we learned about adoptions by some of the other couples who had begun the process with us. One couple reported that they had happily adopted nine year-old twins who were doing very well. The twins, a boy and a girl, were thrilled to have their own swimming pool, while their parents enjoyed buying groceries, shopping for clothes, and having family gatherings. A cozy feeling of satisfaction came over us. We were hopeful.

Another couple had adopted a baby boy who cried considerably and proved to be quite trying for his parents. This mother was getting professional help in order to cope with the stress. She was very depressed at the time. Perhaps the purpose of her report was to warn the rest of us not to expect a life of family bliss after an adoption. It was good for us to see both possibilities. We wondered why she was so depressed, and although she never really made it clear, my feeling was that she was overwhelmed by the baby's many needs. They informed us to expect to need professional help with our parenting of adopted children, and this proved to be good advice.

At another meeting, a young man in his late teens told a story of moving in and out of foster homes until he was finally adopted at the age of fifteen. Many of his problems in foster homes were related to his deep longing for a permanent home. We were thrilled to see how appreciative this young man was for having been adopted. His well-groomed dark curly hair and fair skin free of blemishes gave the impression that someone had been successful at parenting. He was the epitome of what we hoped to do.

This touching story helped Brian and me make the determination to do our best to accept any problems our foster children might have. We wanted to avoid sending a child from home to home. Now we were ready. Our hopes and dreams were as idealistic as any couple waiting for the arrival of its first child. When and who that child might be were the questions uppermost in our minds during several months of waiting.

My Sources of Strength and Courage

My prayer life at this time consisted mostly of Zen meditation with an emphasis during the day on patience. I thought about what it must be like for a pregnant mother and father to wait for the arrival of a baby. Anything can happen; they have to be open to whatever God would give them. So did we. We kept busy and waited for the call from Social Services.

Support from our church community really kept us going. Each Sunday the community asked if there was any news, and their concern was wonderful.

It was very helpful to attend the meetings required by the social services agencies. Not only did we participate with other hopeful parents in important learning, but we heard from both parents and children who had already experienced adoption.

Tips For Adoptive Parents

⤶ When foster parenting, check into adoption early. If not, the foster child you hope to adopt could go to another family on the waiting list.

Books, Music, and Websites

⌐ Adamec, Christine, and William L. Pierce, Ph.D. *The Encyclopedia of Adoption*. New York: Facts On File, 1991. Examines all the social, legal, economic, psychological, and political issues that surround the experience of adoption.

⌐ Melina, Lois Ruskai. RAISING ADOPTED CHILDREN: A Manual for Adoptive Parents. New York: Harper & Row, 1986. Excellent and practical for every imaginable problem—greatly appreciated.

✷ Child Advocates Resource Exchange—features forums, chat, mailing lists, links, and a search area for you to find long-lost parents, children and siblings:

Casey Family Program Homepage: http://www.casey.org/

✷ Foster Parents CARE—provides a list of links to informative sites, parent associations, parents' personal pages, foster agencies, government sites and more: http://www.fostercare.org/

A Baby At Last

3

O ne day the call came. My longing for children was so intense that each detail of the first call has remained a vivid part of my memory. Brian and I were putting up a new patio on the back of our house. I ran to get to the phone before the caller hung up on us.

"Hello," I panted.

"Hello. Is this the Brunner residence?" asked a soft but tense voice.

"Yes, it is," I cautiously replied.

"My name is Carla. I am calling from the protective custody office of Social Services. Would you and your husband be willing to take a two month old Hispanic baby boy into your home for long term foster care?"

My heart jumped into my throat. A baby! This lady had no idea how much we wanted a baby. "Yes, of course, we would love to," I answered easily. "Wait just a moment and I'll ask my husband what he thinks."

I ran outside to tell Brian who was calling, and asked what he thought. "That's what we said. Didn't we?" I ran back to the phone. What a happy day!

As I picked up the phone again, I reached for a pencil and paper to take notes. Then, as Carla began giving me the details

24

of the baby's life-threatening situation, I understood her tense tone and knew that this day was as sad as it was happy. Although I always knew it would have to be this way, the reality of it sickened me. I knew the trauma this baby was experiencing would affect his behavior the rest of his life. If this baby were ever available for adoption, he would be very challenging to raise. I needed to calm myself. I was looking too far ahead.

It seemed this innocent child had been conceived while his mother was on the rebound from a divorce with her husband. She was, in fact, having intimate relations with several men. She wasn't certain which one was the baby's father, and the men were all angry with her for this. One of them threatened her life if she did not name the baby after him, and although it later turned out he was not the father, she named the baby after him to save herself.

This angry man also drove Chris's mother when she had to get to the hospital. Unfortunately, Chris was born on the way to the hospital, in the back seat. The boyfriend yelled, "Kill him. Kill him," and turned into a farm they were passing. Chris's mother screamed, "No! Get us to the hospital." The farmer saw the seriousness of the situation and pulled the driver out of the car. He then got in and drove the new baby and his mother to the hospital.

After they returned home, his mother's ex-husband and father of four older children just wanted out of the mess. Both of the other men said they were determined to kill the baby in order to spite his mother.

During a violent, drunken fight the baby had been thrown under a bed and the police were called. The baby was six weeks old at the time of the fight. At least his mother cared enough

Momther I Love You

about his life to call for help. When the police came, the baby and his two half-sisters were placed in the care of Social Services protective custody. The two boyfriends vowed to find and kill the baby no matter where he was taken. He was in a foster home for temporary care for sixteen days. How awful! Dear God, how could this happen? I had to remember the rule of karma. Bad things do happen to innocent people.

Brian was stunned and silent. How could two grown men want to kill a baby—a completely helpless baby? It staggered his imagination. Carla told me to come the next day to pick him up at his temporary foster home. Then reality hit again, and we realized that we had nothing ready for a baby because we didn't know what age our first child would be. We quickly made some phone calls and got baby things lined up for the next day.

We were instructed to visit with a Social Services supervisor first. She gave us a review of the life histories we had sent her, and discussed with us how having a foster family might impact our lives. I had a terrible time sitting still with her. All I could think of was our baby. Then we were shown to Carla's office. Carla was gracious and direct, and seemed as anxious as we to get to the baby's needs. She was mostly concerned about his safety and care. She told us that his name was Christopher Joseph—my oldest brother's name exactly, which was an interesting coincidence. And Chris was born on my birthday. My heart jumped at the thought—maybe this baby was a gift for us from heaven. Now I am convinced Chris was meant to come to our home from the day of his birth. I remember Carla saying, "for long term foster care." We were going to have a baby; we were both happy and eager to see him, even though we realized his traumatic start in life had to mean he would be a disturbed baby.

26

Chris's caseworker, Carla, was very ashamed to admit that she had been in an accident with Chris after picking him up from his home. "Chris's mother's boyfriends threatened me and I couldn't shake the fear. I'm sorry." A thorough examination at the hospital found him to be free of injury. She wanted us to know that Chris was quite traumatized by the accident and would probably be fussy for a while. Although she didn't want to alarm us, she wanted us to understand how threatening Chris's mother's boyfriends were. "If an Hispanic man comes to your door, don't open it. Call the police."

After a half-hour of sharing information, Carla concluded, "Chris's mother said that she never wanted to see him again. But she could have said this out of frustration. We will be encouraging her to begin visits with Chris and his two sisters as soon as possible. When these visits are set up, I'll give you a call and explain where to bring him." Brian and I agreed that this would be fine without imagining the consequences.

She gave us directions to his foster home and one last warning: "watch for the violent boyfriends." Brian was not as concerned about the boyfriends as I was because he could see no way for them to know where we lived. He was correct. No one ever showed up on our doorstep, but I was not able to shake the fear that one of them might find us for over a year.

Chris's foster mother, Joanne, answered the door with a sweet, welcoming smile. Their home was a haven for troubled teens, but they agreed to take Chris in during the middle of the night because of his urgent need of rescue. They were eager for someone who wanted a baby to take Chris, because he required more time and attention than they were able to continue giving.

After we entered the front door we found ourselves in a hallway leading to the kitchen, and walking past the living room where Chris was. As we passed I saw him. My heart was pounding so fast I could scarcely breathe. Joanne had him lying on a soft white blanket in the middle of the living room floor, where he was kicking and waving his arms at the sun shining through the shutters. I could hear the very climactic music of the 1812 Overture in my mind. Joanne took us straight to the kitchen for feeding instructions. The occasion was huge for us, but just business as usual in the foster care program for them.

"My husband is at work and would appreciate being able to see Chris off, if you don't mind," Joanne requested.

"Of course not. We just need enough time to get all of the necessary baby things for him before bedtime tonight. Chris is our first foster child. We both grew up in large families and have taken care of children as babysitters, but we need all the information you can give us about Chris. He is so young and has had such a very hard start."

"Actually, he is doing much better already. When he came, he cried most of his waking moments. He would even cry in the middle of taking his bottle. Now, he eats well and sleeps for seven hours at night." After sharing these details of his care she asked if we would think of adopting Chris if he should become adoptable.

Nodding my head with a smile, I longingly looked back toward Chris. She understood, and picked him up to hand to me saying, "I'm glad you're willing to adopt him if you can." Brian and I sat on the sofa as she placed him in my arms. The joy of that moment has been a part of me ever since. Brian looked at me and held out his arms for Chris. I carefully handed the baby to him. His ecstasy was written all over his face. We were parents. Chris needed us and we would do anything to help him have his chance in life. It didn't matter at this time if we were foster parents or future adoptive parents.

We were ready to leave when Joanne's husband arrived home from work. He said a tearful goodbye to Chris, and wished him a life of happiness. I saw how quickly these needy children nestle into the hearts of their foster families. Even the foster teenagers came to say goodbye to Chris and to check if we were willing to adopt him, if possible.

As we drove away Chris began to cry. We were strangers to him. Nothing we said or did comforted him. We had made previous arrangements to stop at the home of friends and pick up much needed baby things. This family of former students played with Chris and tired him enough to help him fall asleep. We were grateful.

We knew that babies grip the fingers of their parents. Each time we tried this he simply kept his hands open and limp. He had had too many changes in caregivers to trust us. After six weeks he began gripping our fingers. He was happy and trusting, and I wondered how many more problems he might be able to outgrow.

Chris, shortly after he came to us

Babies have many physical problems that parents and pediatricians try to alleviate. Chris had chronic diarrhea and severe congestion, and both of these problems turned out to be due to an allergy to dairy products. I suspected this when I noticed that his eyes got bloodshot and he sneezed after taking his dairy formula. After explaining this to his pediatrician, the doctor decided to give a dairy-free diet a try. What a difference! Chris could breathe freely and no longer cried after feedings. His joy and ours knew no bounds.

Sometimes I would be lost in serious thought as I cared for Chris. Brian and I often talked about what would happen to him if he ever had to go back to his mother. Chris would notice our sadness and make us smile by laughing and kicking. "What a treasure he is," I thought. Holding him to my cheek, I prayed for him to become adoptable. His mother and father would have to relinquish their parental rights, I knew. If only they knew how happy he was. Brian and I both prayed that no harm would come to him.

My Sources of Strength and Courage

My prayer life at this time involved a constant struggle to shake the baggage of fear. I was meditating each morning and finding myself anxiously checking the front door for possible armed Hispanic men.

It was helpful for me to pray out loud as I took care of Chris. I prayed for our family's safety the same way my mother always prayed for us when we were in danger. Her prayer was: "Jesus, Mary, and Joseph protect us." Once as a child on our farm, I was on a wagon with run-a-way horses. My family came rushing out of the house when they heard the horses, and my mother screamed this prayer. One of my brothers jumped onto the wagon with me and pulled on the reins telling the horses to stop. As a child I had complete confidence that I would be all right, and I was. This same feeling that Chris would be protected

30

made me feel safe as I went about my usual chores. What a gift my mother's faith has been for me and my family.

Although Chris was a foster child, deep down inside I believed that we would adopt and raise him as a bright and happy little boy. I just had to be willing to wait for the system to run its necessary course. I would go around the house with Chris in my arms singing the song of Jesus' Mother, "Let it be."

Sharing joys and fears was a big part of my outgoing nature. I kept calling and visiting my family and friends. We all prayed together for Chris's safety and well being. This community support was crucial. It gave me the strength and courage I needed at the time.

Chris's daily diary helped remind me of his positive growth. Each day of love and healthy response to his needs made him stronger and happier. He was absorbing our spirit of caring, and it would always be his. Nothing could keep me from loving him with all my heart, and my joy was being transferred to him day by day.

I believe that every positive action is a prayer. Each day, all day, I pray—except when I get sidetracked by things like impatience, anger, and quick judgment of others. Then my own lack of peace makes me uncomfortable and I center myself again with the mantra, "I am Veronica. I am breathing." This helps me to be in control again, and life continues as a prayer.

Tips For Adoptive Parents

← Keep note paper ready to jot down questions for counselors—invaluable later.

Books, Music, and Websites

~ Adamec, Christine. *The Complete Idiot's Guide to Adoption.* New York: Alpha Books of Simon and Schuster Macmillan Company, 1998. Can be helpful for clearing foggy issues.

~ *The Bible.* Confraternity New Edition, Imprimatur : Francis Cardinal Spellman, Archbishop of New York 1957. Published by Catholic Book Publishing, New York. I used a quote from this Bible. It is from Matthew Chapter 18 verse 5 "And whoever receives one such little child for my sake, receives me." From the time I heard this as a child until now this is one of my favorite verses from the Bible.

✖ Michele Stanley Parenting Resource Page—created by a non-profit organization for the support and extension of foster care; explains the needs of foster children and provides resources for families: http://ftp.southeast.net/~mstanley/parent.htm

The Special World of Foster Parents

Chris's two sisters had a different foster mother, Mrs. Rand. We met one day when we brought the children to Social Services for a visit with their mother. I learned that his sisters had been in foster care many times before. His mother did not seem to understand that children require complete care for many years. When she was overwhelmed or stressed by them, there would be a big fight and Social Services would be called. Chris's mother asked for Mrs. Rand by name to take care of her children. Caseworkers knew his mother so well, they just called Mrs. Rand and asked if she could take the children again. She knew Chris's whole family, and had foster-parented all four of his mother's children several times. They were all bright children.

Mrs. Rand told me Chris's mother had a volunteer helper during her pregnancy with him. She gave me the volunteer's name, address, and phone number because she knew the volunteer wanted to know about Chris and would be glad to hear from me.

As soon as I got home from Chris's visit with his mother I called Marion, the volunteer. When she found out where Chris was she came right over to see him and offered to help me in any way she could. Her moral support helped me through some trying times later. Marion was relieved to know he was safe. She said she had been so afraid for his life, because of the violent boyfriends, that she had prepared a nursery in her own home to rescue him if necessary. Unfortunately, when Social Services discovered this, they asked Marion to discontinue her services. This whole experience with Chris's mother and Social Services was very upsetting to her.

Social Services may have made a mistake in dismissing Marion. If she had been there when Chris was born, he might not have been so traumatized. Marion, instead of one of the violent boyfriends, could have driven Chris's mother to the hospital.

Abuse due to poverty and alcohol had been in Chris's family for generations. Marion said his mother seemed to feel unloved if she was not being abused. She left a good, kind husband for cruel and abusive boyfriends. This was shocking to Brian and me. If she should ever want Chris back, and should continue to see violent men, he would not stand much of a chance for survival, let alone of having a nurturing childhood.

Now what we wondered was if the system would be as considerate of Chris's needs as it most likely would be of his mother's whimsical demands? As the weeks passed many of Chris's visits were cancelled by his mother. I was advised by our pediatrician to keep a detailed diary about Chris, as it could prove to be helpful later. Judges and psychologists need facts in order to decide what is in the best interest of the child.

Thanksgiving and Christmas were filled with family, friends, and lots of joy. It was difficult to think of Chris as a foster child. His caseworker said he would be in long-term foster placement, but what did that mean to them? For a baby, a month is a long time; for an adult it is short. We felt as if we were in limbo with him. We were naturally bonding with him, but every time he visited with his mother she kept saying to Chris, "You know you're my baby, don't you?" We treated him the same as if we had adopted him. Carla, his caseworker, could not understand why we loved him so much. My parents flew over a thousand miles to share in our joy. What a Christmas!

I was surprised by the satisfaction I felt with this visit from my parents. They now saw and shared our home for the first time. They were also a part of my sense of fulfilling my dreams of parenting. I wanted to be able to do my own thing, but I also wanted to share my new life with my parents. They were happy for me, and my joy was complete as far as my relationship with them was concerned. This meant a lot for my own inner peace and my ability to cope with whatever the future held for our family.

Brian and I enjoyed each of Chris's new developmental steps. He learned to roll over, crawl, feed himself, walk, and talk. He was a happy baby. Taking lots of pictures and placing them around the house was a particularly good "helpful hint" from our home study person. We shared the pictures and portraits of Chris with his mother. She could see that he was happy and she was grateful. When she could, she gave him toys and baby clothes. We kept these for him as keepsakes, in the event that he would stay with us and later might want something from his mother. We chose to not think about the day when he might have to go back to his mother.

After Chris had been with us for two months, we received a call from a different caseworker asking if we would be able to take two more foster children from another family. She said they were sisters and were about two and four. I felt ready to add to our foster family, but Brian didn't. We compromised and agreed to take one of the girls, even though I felt terrible about separating them. My own sister and I had been so close in childhood. I pleaded with Brian, but he insisted on just one. He proved to be right, as usual. These children had mountains of problems. The two together would have been too difficult for me to manage along with baby Chris. I told myself that I would think about taking the other sister in a few months, when I had adjusted to having two foster children.

Jean, our caseworker for the family of the girls, was great. She wished we could take both girls, but understood Brian's reservations about too many too soon. She said she would find another home for the sister. I needed to choose now. What a big decision to make so quickly! Thinking about Chris being so young, I chose the older sister in hopes that she would be more independent. She gave me the phone number of the emergency foster home that had the little girls. Jean had informed me these foster parents were eager to have the children placed in more permanent foster homes. So, once again we could make someone happy and satisfy our own desire for children.

"Hello," said a sweet but tired voice of an older lady.

"Hello, Myrna, my name is Veronica Brunner. I'm calling about one of your foster children."

"Oh, no. We have two sisters. You can't separate them," she half insisted.

"We were just informed by Jean, their caseworker, that we could," I explained. "I've decided to take care of the four-year-old, Cathie. Jean asked me to tell you to call her back about the younger sister, Jenny." I felt guilty as I gave the information.

"Well, all right," Cathie's foster mother said. "You sound new at this foster parenting. I certainly hope you don't think you are going to change the parents of these children. They are beyond hope. I saw them bring a grocery cart with four children in it right into our church and beg for money to buy milk for them. The children smelled so bad and were so dirty that we could scarcely breathe near them. I could smell cigarettes and booze as they went past me. Our pastor felt pity for the children and gave them ten dollars for milk. My guess is those kids never got the milk," she emphatically concluded.

What? Trying to correct the parents had never even occurred to me. "I hadn't thought about the parents," I meekly replied. "You can bring Cathie over any time after 4:30 this afternoon. I'll prepare supper for us. Thank you." I hung up—a bit stunned.

Several weeks earlier, Brian and I had read an article in the paper about an appalling situation where children were found unattended in an apartment. There was a picture of a fecal-strewn room. The police had taken the children. Social Services would place the children in foster homes. Jean informed us that Cathie was one of these children.

What were we getting ourselves into with this family? The challenge of foster parenting was getting more exciting. If Cathie's parents were the kind of people her foster mother was convinced they were, she might be different from any child I ever knew. This could be a big problem for me. In the past I had cared for children according to the wishes of their parents. Obviously, that was out. How would I know what to do for a child I could not comprehend? What had her life been like so far? I wondered how she would act in a nice clean home where I would be watching her almost every waking minute. Nothing could have prepared me for the next four years with Cathie. She was fortunate that Brian and I wanted a family very much, and that I thrived on meeting challenges.

My Sources of Strength and Courage

Each new experience with Social Services was food for thought and prayer. We constantly challenged the unjust and cruel ways children were treated by the system. My father had taught me to speak my mind. He always did, and all thirteen of us knew it. So I automatically did the same. I don't know what changes have taken place because of my criticism or exchange of ideas, but I was told that they are many. In my thinking, this is all prayer. This is what Jesus did in his time, now it was my turn to let Jesus live on in me.

I have always enjoyed the story of Jesus and the children. In Matthew's Gospel Jesus said, "Whoever receives one such little child for my sake, receives me" (Matt. 18: 5). Children naturally enjoy life if they are given the chance. Their different cultures and backgrounds don't matter to them at all. They all want to play and have fun. I have a beautiful picture of Jesus with children of different nationalities that I used on my classroom bulletin boards for years. Now I used it in my own home to help my family understand God's love for all of us. I put it on the wall in Chris's bedroom. Chris was Hispanic. We loved him just as he was, but what about the rest of society? I had to hope and pray that he would be accepted. Our own love and acceptance of him would be an example for our neighbors and school friends. We openly loved him and shared his progress everywhere we went.

But I found that my own prayerful life could not make up for the lack of it in the first years of Cathie's life. Both children came from homes where alcohol and cigarettes used up a great deal of the family income. Although Cathie was unable to talk much, she did communicate with Chris by pushing his swing, and running to tell me what she thought his needs were. This was fine until I realized one day that Cathie was quite deceitful. She was in her own world of survival for a four-year-old. She learned to say and do whatever pleased her parents. Truth did not matter. She had to avoid her father's anger at all costs. I realized she would pass this on to Chris. It was unavoidable.

I began telling Cathie the stories of Jesus. She found solace in the fact that Jesus suffered even though He didn't deserve it. But she never understood honesty. I had to accept this as the direct result of her parents' ignorance and neglect, along with abuse in their own childhoods. We would have to patiently wait until Cathie and Chris were old enough to explain the evil of deceit. No amount of prayer could erase this. As I meditated on this, I came to realize that every little bit of goodness Cathie absorbed from me would crowd out the harm done in her early years, little by little. For the time being that was the best that I could do.

Cathie had the gift of being able to copy what she saw. She learned more by copying than by any other method. I knew that I would have to talk a lot about goodness as well as have her listen to and sing happy, positive songs. The road ahead was a long one. I had a lot of time. I knew my years of experience as a primary teacher and as a religion teacher could be just what Cathie needed, and, of course, God knew that all along. That was why she was with us.

Tips For Adoptive Parents

✦ Unless we enter into a child's world of suffering, we have no right to be his or her parent.
✦ Foster children never forget their brothers and sisters. If possible, take them to see each other often.

Books, Music, and Websites

— Komar, Miriam, D.S.W. *Communicating With the Adopted Child*. New York: Walker & Company Publishing 1991. Helpful with much-needed honesty.
❧ FosterLove—this compilation of resources, created by a foster parent, provides links to many relevant support services. It includes info on attachment issues: http://www.fosterlove.com/

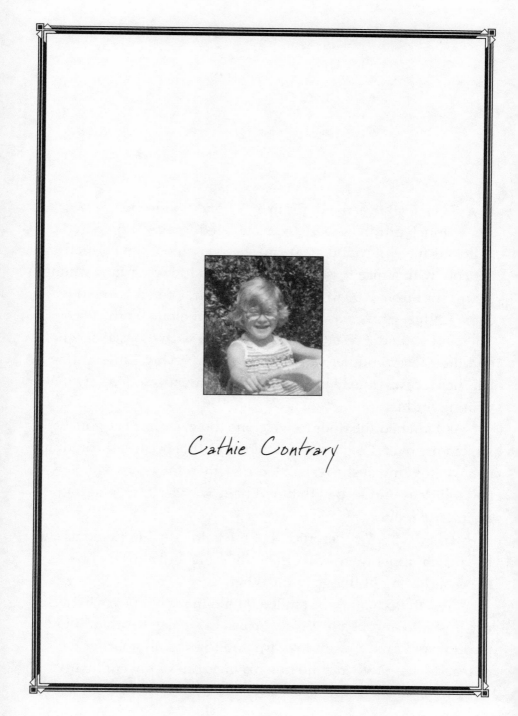

Cathie Contrary

5

When Cathie arrived, Brian and I had no idea just how much our lives were to be changed forever. I prepared a delicious meal of round steak, mashed potatoes, and corn on the cob, with a nice tossed salad. Brian had to work the evening swing shift from 3:00 to 11:00, so he couldn't be with me to welcome Cathie. Chris was sound asleep. I sat alone by the window and waited. Presently an automobile with the two sisters and their foster mother turned into our driveway. Little Cathie had her face anxiously pressed to the car window. She saw me waiting for her.

As I opened the door to welcome them, Cathie cautiously looked me over. I must have stared at Cathie because I couldn't believe how much she resembled me when I was her age. She had a little round face with blond hair. She was thin, and had an intense look.

"Hi, Myrna. I'm Veronica. Let me help you," I offered as she tried with difficulty to walk in holding one little girl by one hand and a bag of things in the other.

"Yes, thank you," she smiled. "I am in such a hurry because my husband and I have a New Year's Eve party to attend in just a couple of hours. I want to warn you to keep all your food out of reach. These two just ate five bananas out of my cupboard.

Maybe they will be better off if they are separated. They were hard for me to keep up with," she confessed. "They have a new young caseworker. You have to keep her on her toes or she'll forget about you."

First parents and now caseworkers; Myrna seemed to want to control the lives of lots of people. Kids were all that I could manage for now. I loved it. "Are the girls potty trained?" I asked as she placed them on our beautiful flowered living room chair and sofa.

"Oh, I think so," she said with enough doubt in her voice to prompt me to quickly suggest that we all stand as she explained how she had been caring for Cathie so far. I was quite concerned about how we were going to separate these two precious little sisters. Jenny, almost two, clung to Myrna with so much fear and bashfulness I decided to give my attention to Cathie. I looked at Myrna and said, "Maybe Cathie would like to see the rest of the house."

"O.K. you show Cathie her new foster home," said Myrna as she began to talk to Jenny. "I'll show you your new foster home too."

Cathie took my hand shyly and looked back at Jenny as I began the grand tour. As soon as we were out of sight, I heard the front door close. Myrna had left with Jenny. I felt terrible again for separating two sisters. Cathie was totally uninterested in our house. When we went into the narrow, compact kitchen to get Cathie's supper, and she looked into the empty living room, I saw big tears silently running down her cheeks. There had to be a better way to handle this difficult situation.

"You will get to see Jenny again," I assured Cathie, picking her up and placing her on the kitchen counter beside the food.

43

"Do you like corn?" I asked as I put food on her plate. She silently nodded her head. So far, she didn't talk. I thought she needed time to adjust to so much newness in her life. I didn't have to wait for long to hear her voice. When I placed the plate of food in her hands, her eyes got big and she slurred out her first words to me.

"Zis is aw zor me?" she asked clinging to the plate as if someone might snatch it from her. "No ody zill tae ziss zrom me?"

"Yes, you can eat all of it," I answered. "Who would take it from you if you were with your family?"

"My mommy and daddy," she answered. Then I helped her put her plate on the table in the dining room and get up on the chair. I went back to the kitchen to get my own plate of food. It could not have taken more than five seconds. When I got to the table to sit down, she had already eaten her mashed potatoes with her fingers. She did not even notice the silverware. I began to eat my potatoes with a fork. She did not even look at me. Her eyes were riveted on the food and she ate as if she had not had anything for days. Myrna said she had just polished off several bananas before she came, and I was sure that they would have eaten regular meals for the past weeks.

I wondered what kind of life she was accustomed to living. At this point, I thought of her stay with us as temporary. I wasn't sure if her past life was any of my concern. But I did feel that as long as she was with us, she should do as we did. No four-year-old was going to eat like an animal at our table. When I showed her how to eat with a fork, she smiled and copied me. I sensed that she liked the attention of being taught. I was grateful that I had been a primary teacher.

With supper finished, I prepared her for bed. Since we had no extra beds upstairs—only in the basement of our blond brick, ranch-style home—I made up the love seat for her. It was in the family room where we all spent a lot of time. She had no nightclothes. In fact, when I looked into her paper bag, I found only a clown doll and a ragged stuffed rabbit. Myrna told me their clothes were so dirty they had to be destroyed. The clothes she was wearing were hand-sewn by Myrna.

While I filled the tub for her bath, she stayed about three inches from me. After explaining that the bath water was for her, I began helping her get undressed. She did not like being washed. The bath was frightening to her. I learned later her father had tried to drown her older brother on two occasions. She had a diaper rash from her waist to her knees. As I washed the bottoms of her feet, I saw what looked like pinholes over the entire surfaces. I knew we needed to see our pediatrician as soon as possible.

I shared some of my nightclothes with her for this first night. Although I laughed at how funny she looked in my shirt, Cathie didn't. She remained silent and uninterested. Once she was tucked in, she looked so angelic that I got my camera for a picture. She did not smile, but looked blankly at the camera as if she had never seen one before.

"Would you like me to read a story to you, Cathie?" I got another blank stare. I was beginning to realize that Cathie had had extremely limited experiences. Holding up her doll and stuffed rabbit, I asked, "Which one do you want to sleep with you?" She reached up and emphatically snatched the doll from me as if she needed to protect it.

After reading to her and turning out the light I sat on the floor beside her. Much to my surprise she was sound asleep in just a few minutes. I could not even hear her breathing. I sat on the full sized couch across the room from her. The kitchen light filtered into the darkness. I could make out her precious little round face snuggled up to her clown doll. Now she looked like a peaceful child. When she was awake, she had the worried look of a thirty-year-old woman with the weight of the world on her alone. I discovered that this is true of many foster children. They are forced to grow up too soon just in order to survive.

Shortly after Cathie fell asleep, Brian called. "Has Cathie arrived yet? What does she look like?"

"Yes, she is here sound asleep on our love seat. She is very tiny with brown eyes and blond hair. She can't talk much. And she has only one set of clothes. I'll have to take her shopping tomorrow and get some for her. Jean knew she would need clothes. She said that Social Services would pay for them."

"I sure hope this isn't a mistake," he said.

"How can it be?" I asked. "We wanted a family. We may not be going to adopt these two, but they certainly are needy children and we are taking care of them. If this isn't family, I don't know what is." I hung up with a happy heart. But I thought of Brian, and his position in all of these events. He had to be at work in order to keep open all the possibilities of having a family at all. He wanted to be home with me as our family changed. What a wonderful man! I thanked God for all that was happening in our lives.

The next morning I happily got up to take care of Chris with his usual routine. After a very long sleep, Cathie got up quietly and came to me without a word. I cheerfully greeted her, only to get another blank stare. I chatted away about breakfast and going shopping—no response. I placed a bowl of cereal in front of her and showed her how to use a spoon. She used it.

"Cathie, now that breakfast is over, it is time for you to meet our baby," I said. She followed me to Chris's nursery. Chris was awake and excited to see another child. Cathy was blank once again. I know now that she could not understand where her baby brother, Tommy, was. He was almost killed in a drunken fight between her parents, and she was worried about him. She immediately wanted to give Chris his bottle. In fact, each time Chris gave the slightest little cry, Cathie came to me saying, "Boll zor aeby." After deciphering what she meant, I had to explain that Chris did not always want a bottle if he cried. Sometimes he just needed some exercise in his swing or to be talked to for a while, or carried around the house for exploring. She gave me the impression that this was all new and good. She liked it.

I don't think Cathie was talked to very much at all. She had no idea how to play either. Maybe her parents did not know that children needed more than food. Wow! There was no end to her mountain of needs, and I would have to fulfill these for her one need at a time. Before I met Brian I had already climbed several real mountains. That had seemed impossible, too. But I did it, and together Brian and I could help Cathie climb over her mountain of problems, too. It depended on how long she could stay with us.

When Brian came to the dining room for breakfast, I cheerfully introduced him to Cathie. Brian automatically picked her up. She liked his gentle, kind attention. She smiled. I was relieved because I knew that many foster children have had abusive fathers, and are therefore afraid of men. After holding Cathie a few minutes, Brian asked her if she wanted to go shopping. She gave her usual blank look. She most likely didn't know what the word meant. I explained that she needed some clothes to wear. We could go to the store and buy some for her. Her eyes lit up and she smiled. There were many bargains in the stores because of New Year's Day clearances. Brian agreed to stay home with Chris while I shopped with Cathie. We filled the shopping cart with clothes and a few toys. I took for granted that she needed a coat. I tried several on her and found a good fit and put it in the cart. I saw the blank look again. I don't think she ever owned a coat. I repeated the word for her many times because she kept pointing to it wanting to know its name.

When we got home with all the clothes and toys, Cathie was both delighted and bewildered. We put the clothes in a closet and took the toys to our large basement playroom. She just sat on the floor and looked at them. I began to play house with her. I ironed with a little play iron over some doll clothes. "Now it is your turn, Cathie." She silently imitated me. "Yes you are ironing the clothes," I told her. Once she did something she wanted to repeat it many times. I was happy for her and I wanted her to stay and continue playing. I tried to leave quietly, but she grabbed up all the toys she could carry and followed me.

For the next two weeks I took care of Chris and did my household chores with Cathie always at my side. Her clown doll was her constant companion. When left to her own world, she chattered and babbled very fast. "Be zooo, Shennie! Tae boll, Tommy. No zry. Teve, wet me wone!" Eventually I could understand it. She was telling her little sister, Jenny, to be good; her baby brother, Tommy, to take his bottle and stop crying; and her big brother, Steve, to let her alone. She said each thing with such grown up seriousness that one would think she felt responsible for all of them.

Wanting to relieve Cathie of her worry, I began to talk to her about her brother and sister. "Cathie, you will not have to take care of Jenny and Tommy any more."

"No more Jenny and Tommy," she said with what sounded to me like a sigh of relief. Then she walked into the bathroom and stood in front of the toilet stool and deliberately wet her clothes and the floor. I had upset rather than helped her. She was thinking about them because she wanted to know how they were, not because she had to take care of them. Now she refused to use the toilet at all. She began urinating and defecating anywhere. She was very frustrated, and so was I.

Her caseworker told me to feel free to call her any time so I decided to take her up on it. Much to my surprise, Jean was absolutely wonderful. She was happy to know that we cared so much about Cathie. "You have probably given her more attention in the short time you have had her than she has had in her entire life with her parents," she said.

As I continued to relate to Jean all that was going on, I could feel myself relaxing. Now I understood why she told me to call anytime. This unburdening was much better than bottling up my frustration, which might end in a move for Cathie to a different foster home. At the time there was no solution to Cathie's frustration. Her whole family was in turmoil. I told her I talked to her caseworker and that her brothers and sister were all right. I promised again that she would see them soon. She was very unhappy with the waiting. It took a cherry pie to get her mind off of them.

Cathie began weekly visits with her family that were carefully monitored by Jean behind a one-way window. She informed me that each week Cathie would go in to see her parents, only to be disappointed again and again by their lack of interest in her. They only responded to the two youngest children. Cathie would play with her big brother for a short time and then lay on the floor kicking and crying for attention. When this didn't work, she would put on her coat and stand by the door waiting to leave. Jean's guess was that Cathie was probably eager for attention from us, since she was being ignored by her parents.

When I heard this I felt so much sympathy for Cathie that I was more eager than before to take care of her. At this point, she had not thrown any tantrums for us. I felt good about her wanting our love and attention.

My Sources of Strength and Courage

With so much joy and family satisfaction in my heart, prayers of gratitude permeated my spirits. We all attended Church about five miles away. Our friends there were interested in our foster children's lives and prayed with us for their safety and future happiness.

The most difficult aspect to deal with now was the uncertainty. Would their parents get themselves together and provide for their children's needs? Would the judge understand the needs of the children or just think of the adults? I prayed for the ability to think clearly for the sake of the children myself. At church we asked the community to pray for wisdom for the judge.

Prayers for safety were in big order now. Cathie was very active. I was never sure of what to expect from her quick movements. This must be why the Guardian Angel prayer was such a big thing in my childhood. As a child, I had great faith in the protection of my Guardian Angel, whom I named Marty. So it was only natural for me to trust the Angels of these two precious little children to watch over them. I prayed for them to my own Marty, and went about my chores in peace.

Brian and I were blessed in having been raised by such good parents. We were both from Christian families, just different denominations. This was not a source of contention for us at all. We had the same basic beliefs and went to church together, where we respectfully participated in the services. I enjoyed being a lector and a Eucharistic minister. That was fine with Brian.

I could always sense when I needed time away for spiritual replenishment. In the convent I had experienced annual retreats. My spiritual clock just told me when I was in need again. This idea was foreign to Brian. He couldn't understand it. His mother had never taken time away from him that he could remember. But I insisted, and he co-operated by taking care of the children for a couple of days. Sometimes I made a retreat with the women from our church. Other times I went to our trailer by the lake for peace and quiet and time to read. When I came home from these mini vacations I felt like a new person. My patience and understanding were increased because I had time to appreciate all that I was experiencing with them. I discovered that gratitude for them was one of my biggest helps in accepting their problems. It kept me in a positive frame of mind and made the family happier.

Tips For Adoptive Parents

↵ As soon as negative feelings toward the child surface, voice this to a stable helper.

↵ If children can be prevented from overhearing phone conversations about their past, it should be done.

Books, Music, and Websites

— Bunin, Sherry and Catherine. *Is That Your Sister?* New York: Pantheon Books, Knopf Publishing Group 1976. Helpful for families of different races.

✶ FosterLove—this compilation of resources, created by a foster parent, provides links to many relevant support services. It includes info on attachment issues: http://www.fosterlove.com/

Brian and I Could Make a
Difference

I could not imagine what it was like to be in Cathie's shoes. Her parents could not take proper care of her, and yet they were all the permanent family she had known. She wanted to be with them. Apparently, two weeks in foster care were usual for her. She seemed to be comfortable with us until now. She began pouting on a daily basis. She walked around the house with her lower lip protruded. She was frustrated. We tried cheering her with humor. Laughing, we teased that we could have a contest to see who could make their lip come out the most. This worked for only a brief time. She found solace in playing with her dolls—they were her family.

Two weeks must have been the magic time for Cathie's parents, also. They now wanted their children back. We received a phone call from a lawyer one day. "Hello, Mrs. Brunner, I am Cathie's Guardian Ad Litem. Her parents are sitting here in front of me and want to have their children. They say their apartment is now clean and ready for them. Do you have anything you want to say about Cathie?"

Social Services neglected to tell us about Guardians Ad Litem. "What do you mean? I have no idea who you are."

"Foster children in protective custody have a court appointed lawyer. I am Cathie's. Do you think Cathie is ready to come back to her parents?"

"No way! With them Cathie must have been living like an animal. She has no idea how to be civilized."

"Oh, thank God for foster parents like you. I am taking notes. Please give me, as thoroughly as you can, all of the reasons for your position on this case."

After I listed the many behavioral problems indicative of almost no parenting, I suggested that her parents be investigated before allowing her to go back. Her lawyer thanked me profusely and assured me that both she and Jean would check out this family.

This protest on my part had a profound effect on Cathie's life and the lives of her brothers and sister. I couldn't believe what I had done. I realized that I may have saved their lives. And, at the same time, I wondered what would ever happen to their family. If I had chosen to send Cathie back, no one would have paid attention to their past. Thank God my father taught me to always expose injustice. I knew no four-year-old child should be as deprived as Cathie was.

About a week later, Jean called to let me know that I was right about Cathie's family. They had a long history of inhuman behavior. Six other children had been taken from these parents. They would need a lot of help to change their patterns and be able to nurture children. In the other cases, they had abandoned their children in foster care. She warned me they most likely would do the same thing this time.

Brian and I were dumbfounded for days. We just couldn't believe parents like these existed. Should we ask to adopt her if her parents left her with us? Although she had only been with us for three short weeks, it was obvious she would be difficult to raise.

Now we found out what trouble was. When Cathie's stay with us extended beyond the usual time span, she was unhappy, to say the least. Brian said, "She must have been in a number of other foster homes, because she was so easy to please for the first two weeks. Now nothing satisfies her." Each morning she sat up in her bed and wet it. She began shredding her clothes. This calculated bad behavior became a habit that remained for years. Each time we showed disapproval, she smirked.

We decided to not focus on her bad behavior because it was too frustrating for us, and Cathie seemed to like upsetting us, after all, it was one of the only ways she could exert some control over her life. I tried desperately to help her be a happy child. Brian and I read to her, put on cheerful children's music, and played with her. Nothing worked. Then one day I realized I was trying to force her to be happy. It just hadn't occurred to me that she had a perfect right to be miserable, whether I liked it or not. However, I was aware that she was definitely wearing down my naturally cheerful disposition, and I resented her for this. Knowing how unhealthy the situation was becoming, I decided to ask Jean for some kind of relief.

I gave her a call. "What do you think would help us get along better?"

"Maybe we could put her in a pre-school a couple of days a week. Would that give you enough of a break?"

"Oh, yes. That would be great! Thank you so much." Cathie was lucky to have such a good caseworker.

Pre-school proved to be more helpful than we imagined. I had time to enjoy Chris again, to sit back and put myself in Cathie's shoes somewhat, and to begin writing a diary for her.

Another huge benefit for her was that while she was there she could forget about her family worries. This made her feel comfortable for two days each week. She also got tested by her teachers. They became interested in her case and spoke with her mother for more information. All of this was helpful later in court—it became an important part of Cathie's case history.

Cathie thrilled to be on her own Big Wheel.

Another big plus for pre-school was that Cathie had been in one previously. Even before putting the children in foster care, social workers were suspicious about the treatment of Cathie and her siblings by their parents. So, as a precaution, they were placed in pre-school. Cathie's experience there was good. She went home to her parents each evening. I gradually became aware of just how much she associated the present school with her first one. Each day she expected to see her birth parents pick her up from school. Instead, it was I. Her face fell each time I came. Once I knew why, I had sympathy for her. Her first experience with pre-school as a positive family memory has remained a blessing for her.

Our family enjoying the backyard shortly before Tommy's arrival.

Something we did not know about foster children was their frustration due to total loss of control in their lives. Ordinarily, a baby learns from routine what to expect next, which gives the child a form of control. But this stability gets lost when parents are not there. Because of this loss, a small child thinks his or her life is in danger. They feel the need to "kill or be killed." Cathie gave us first hand awareness of this phenomenon by trying to kill Chris. One morning after breakfast I put Chris in his walker. Cathie was playing dolls near him in our dining room. They seemed content and safe, so I thought I would quickly run to the bathroom. Just as I was washing my hands, Cathie came to me and said, "Me ill Ris. Ris no me aeby. Me wan me aeby, Tommy."

"Kill Chris? Where?" I asked as I tried to remain calm, even though my heart was in my throat. Cathie always became very upset if I was angry. I held her hand so she couldn't run ahead of me. She took me to him in the family room. She did plan to kill him. She had pushed him in his walker through our kitchen and down one step between the family room and kitchen. There she had placed him right at the top of the stairs to the basement. Chris was fine, happily chewing on his teether.

Thanks to all of our Guardian Angels, Cathie told me before she tried to push him down. She knew we never left Chris in that room because of this danger. The answer was to get a gate immediately and to call Jean.

As much as I dreaded the idea of moving Cathie around to different foster homes, I now feared for Chris's life. So, I asked her, "Do you think maybe Cathie needs to be with more experienced foster parents?"

Much to my surprise, she said, "No, I don't think that would help, but I understand your stress. You just need more knowledge about foster children. Cathie is doing what foster children do. When she said she wanted to kill Chris, she probably just wanted to have her baby brother there because he is familiar. Would you like some information about children with her problems?"

In disbelief of what I had just heard, I managed to say, "I suppose that could help."

"After you read the materials that I'll bring to your home tomorrow, you may feel better equipped to help her. But if not, and you still want to have her moved, I will."

I agreed that I was extremely ignorant about what to expect from Cathie. While waiting for the materials, I wondered if Social Services had deliberately avoided teaching us these "foster children behavior patterns" in order to insure that we would stay in the program. Or, do you suppose they just didn't think about it enough?

As I read the material, I was amazed to discover that abused and neglected children understand their abuse as love. It is usually the only way they experience being touched. When they are removed from this familiar behavior, they are so insecure they do everything possible to recreate the very abuse from which they were rescued in the first place. After reading this and sharing the information with Brian, we decided to accept Cathie the way she was and keep a closer eye on her. Like Jean said, "She is just doing what foster children do."

Her parents continued to visit weekly at Social Services under the watchful eye of Jean. All of the children were picked up by Jean and taken to the visits. There was never any embarrassment as there was with Chris's visits. A good caseworker can make a big difference for everyone involved in the foster care program, especially the children.

It was disconcerting to see how seldom little Cathie smiled. I became aware of her intense loneliness. Now her visits with her parents had to be stopped because they had head lice. The two younger children, who sat on their parents' laps during the visits, returned home with lice, and Social Service personnel asked the parents to be checked. They refused, saying there was no problem. How sad for Cathie.

My Sources of Strength and Courage

Open, open, open, I kept repeating to myself. I needed to open my mind to the new world I was learning about from Cathie. Jesus' mother had had to open her mind and will to an unknown future when she was asked to be His mother. Now we were being asked to do the same.

As I did my chores, I remembered the song "Let It Be." This helped me to stay calm and receptive to any new ideas from Cathie or Social Services. These times were so trying that I sometimes played records from my primary teaching albums. They were meant to teach Christian virtues to children, but I could use them now to sustain me in my own need for virtue. The quality of simplicity was helpful to me. As I listened to and sang these songs repeatedly, Cathie began to join me. I was aware of God constantly working from me to her and vice versa. It was so empowering.

I decided to have her sit quietly and watch me play the piano. This was another form of prayer for me. As a child I had always wished for a piano and lessons, but my parents could not afford them so I had to wait until I could manage it all myself. At 35 I started lessons through the adult education program at the local high school. Then I went on to private lessons. Eventually I was able to play the piano with both hands just as I had admired so many other people doing. I had always wondered how anybody could have one hand playing the melody and the other playing something different. It just seemed impossible to me. So when I learned it, I experienced great gratification.

Now I was playing to sooth myself and Cathie. After watching me do this daily for several weeks, Cathie went to the piano

61

and began playing the same song, "Somewhere My Love," with both hands. I couldn't believe it. My need for prayer in music led to another big discovery. Cathie was superb at copying.

More and more positive developments resulted from decisions to keep on trying to meet her needs. This encouraged me to hang in there and allow God to help her through me.

The reading materials that were eventually given me by Jean, the caseworker, were very useful. There are many good books written about foster children.

Tips For Adoptive Parents

⤙ A child's right to misery needs to be understood and respected, but not encouraged for prolongation.

⤙ Be aware that abused children seek more abuse—this will help you understand the source of their negative behavior.

Books, Music, and Websites

⁀ "Dominique," from *The Singing Nun*, by Crown Records, Los Angeles, CA.

⁀ Bartholet, Elizabeth. *Family Bonds: Adoption and the Politics of Parenting*. New York: Houghton Mifflin Company, 1993. A different look at the meaning of family.

⤚ The City of Foster City—check out FCTV Live! Foster City Update, City Council Planning Commission & Resident Advisory Committees, Civic Center Master Plan/Government Center/Senior Center Updates, Background/Visitor Information, Parks and Recreation: http://www.fostercity.org/

My First Court Experience

1

When Cathie's parents had their day in court, I decided to go. I wanted to see and hear these parents for myself, but realizing how important it was to keep my identity unknown, I first asked Jean if I could be there. She said anyone had the right to go, but to be aware that there was a possibility the judge might ask for my identity. Fortunately, many schoolteachers were going to be there from Cathie's and Steve's schools, and I could easily blend in with them. I wore my sunglasses the whole time. I was nervous, but excited to be there. This was my first experience of any real courtroom procedure.

When I arrived in the hall outside the courtroom, I saw a nervous couple waiting. I later learned they were Cathie's parents. They were both extremely thin. Their clothes were very wrinkled, and Cathie's mother's hair looked as if she had taken curlers out without combing it. They both had teeth missing and spoke with heavy lisps. They looked at me, and I simply looked away.

Many witnesses came in hopes of persuading the judge to keep the children in foster care. Everyone who knew the children and cared about them agreed that these parents would need extensive help before they could get the children back. Would the judge agree? My most pressing curiosity at this time was about the individual characters of her parents. What were they like?

That day proved to be tremendously valuable for understanding Cathie's way of thinking. I can't imagine how else I could have managed all of the turmoil of the next few years. Her parents sat directly in front of me. Each time an accusation was made, they assured their lawyer it was a lie. They maintained their innocence throughout five hours of testimony. Blaming babysitters was their constant strategy. Cathie's mother took the stand and told a long story of her experiences with the children and her relatives. They moved from grandparents to aunts and uncles almost every two months. They didn't want to stay anywhere too long because they didn't want anyone to get mad at them. With a big cut above her right eye, it looked as if she had been in a fight just before she came. I was dumbfounded when she began to boast of surviving Cathie's birth one December.

"We were at a truck stop when I began to have pains. I told John, my husband, that the baby was coming. I needed a doctor. He said we couldn't afford one and I would have to hold the baby in until we got to my mother's home [two hundred miles away]. Me, John, and Steve all got in the truck and kept driving. Then the baby started to come. John stopped along the road and I got out in the ditch. Cathie was born there in the cold. She began to turn blue. I thought we were both going to die. Then some kind folks stopped and put me and the baby in their camper and rushed us to a clinic in the nearest town. John didn't know where they took us. Cathie got put in a baby warmer and she turned pink. I knew she would make it. Three days later John and Steve found us and drug us right out of that clinic because we didn't have no money."

Everyone in the courtroom was stunned. The silence was one of incredulity. Cathie's mother had no idea that she just described an almost barbaric family situation. And yet she spoke with such personal triumph. She seemed proud to have survived in spite of her husband's domineering ignorance, which almost caused her own and Cathie's deaths. Now I understood why Cathie was so strong. She had been surviving under primitive conditions since the day of her birth.

When Cathie's maternal grandmother took the witness stand, she openly admitted that she was happy to hear the four children were getting good care in foster homes. She apologized for not giving Cathie's mother a better upbringing. She told the judge that every time her daughter and son-in-law ran out of money they came to sponge off her. She wished they would settle down in a permanent home. I was relieved to know that someone in the family was aware that the parents had not met the children's needs. I was also gratified to learn that Cathie's grandmother was so honest and perceptive. Maybe someday Cathie would have these same traits.

Then we heard from Cathie's father. I was wondering what he would have to say, since his wife and mother-in-law had not given him good marks for being a responsible husband and father. When the judge asked him to take the stand, John demonstrated an obvious disability. He was unable to find his way to the witness stand. He would come to an obstacle, such as a table, and just stand there as though he couldn't find his way around it. After two unsuccessful attempts, the judge pointed a path from John's seat to the stand. Once on the stand, he was very reluctant to answer any questions. Each response came only after a long pause and empty stares at every person in the room. The judge watched him closely, appearing sympathetic.

John boasted of working ten and twelve hour days at a nearby egg farm. Together with his wife they had a combined income of $400 per week. He drove a semi to deliver eggs. He saw no need for the children to be in foster care. When asked about his children's developmental delays he explained it as just being their nature. Any problems his children might have at this time were due to foster care. They just needed to be with their parents. When asked why Cathie did not have glasses to correct a crossed eye, which was on the verge of going blind, he simply stated that they planned on taking care of it when they had time.

Cathie and Steve's teachers testified about the children's behavior and test results. They both sat silently in corners or fearfully crawled under desks or chairs. Both had emotional problems that would require many years of therapy before they could feel comfortable in an average classroom. Their inability to communicate made their test results invalid. They seemed to be retarded.

Cathie's baby brother, Tommy, had a skull fracture from a blunt object—a fact established by a doctor's interpretation of an x-ray. John blamed the fracture on a baby sitter. Jean gave the information that she had gleaned from Steve and Cathie, knowing full well that it would mean very little to the judge. Seven-year-old Steve had told Jean that his father had kicked baby Tommy in the head. Cathie said that her mother stepped on him.

Years later, when Steve could talk more clearly and he no longer feared telling the truth, he said that his father had come home drunk. Baby Tommy, then nine months old, was asleep on the floor. His father started a fight with his mother, not noticing Tommy until they stepped on him. This angered his father and he kicked Tommy in the head. Then, realizing from Steve's screams that Tommy was unconscious and blue, they decided to take him to the hospital in a city fifteen miles away, instead of the one in their own city. To compound the medical emergency, when they tried to get all four children into the vehicle, the baby was accidentally dropped on his head into the gravel. They then decided to leave the three older children at the apartment, with seven year old Steve in charge.

After arriving at the hospital, Tommy's parents handed him to the emergency room personnel with the comment, "We think he is sick." Tommy was unconscious, blue, very feverish, covered with bruises, and filthy. As soon as Tommy was stabilized, one of the nurses questioned the parents about their other children. When they said there were three more children in their apartment in another city, the police were called to check on them.

According to the police report, it was a cold night in December. The children were asleep in the smelly, fecal-strewn apartment's living room. Steve was in a sleeping bag on the floor just six inches from an open flame gas heater. Four-year-old Cathie, and Jennie, almost two, were sleeping on the couch. Their clothes were soaked with urine and feces. The police woke the children and explained that they were going to find warm, clean homes for them. They were taken to the police station where they waited several hours while Social Services found foster homes for them.

Seven-year-old Steve was placed in a teen group home. He was so unruly, smearing feces on the bathroom walls and running all over the house destroying things, that it was suggested that he be placed in an institution for the mentally ill. However, after phone calls to several foster homes, he was given a chance. He did well and stayed in the group home. Cathie and Jenny were placed together in a temporary foster home—the very same foster home from which Cathie was delivered to us about three weeks later.

As I sat in court that day, it occurred to me that these parents might be too ignorant to be helped by Social Services. I hoped to be able to adopt Cathie someday and give her a chance to be a happy person. But I knew that her parents could give Social Services minimal cooperation and still get the children back, to return to their usual way of life, neglect and abuse.

According to the court reports, the family lived in their truck camper in a city park while their mother served time in jail for theft. No one could understand why they were stealing, and not providing the necessities for their children, when they were earning enough money to do so. Babysitters testified that the children were always unwashed, and that the parents refused to pay for their services. Naturally, the babysitters stopped coming. The children were then left on their own all day without food and sometimes without water. A police officer testified that on one occasion, when they lived in a trailer park, he had been called by neighbors to come one night and insist that the children be allowed to enter the trailer. They were locked out in the cold without sufficient clothing.

At the end of all this testimony, the judge floored me by saying, "The abnormal behavior of the children in the classrooms is indicative of serious neglect. They will remain in foster care in this county." Then he told the parents they were required to pay the county for the foster care of their children, pass a parenting skills test, and cooperate with Social Services with visitation privileges. Cathie's parents complied only with the last of these. They agreed to take parenting classes but never showed up for them.

Walking out of court that day my head and heart were aching for a vacation. I was dizzy and had to sit in my car for a while before I was able to safely drive home. During the fifteen-mile drive home I reflected on the appalling world of Cathie and her family. They lived only a few miles from our home, in our own city. How could our lives be so different?

According to their family histories, both of Cathie's parents, as children, had been raised the same way they were now treating their own children. If we didn't stop the cycle, it would be passed on to another generation. I wished that Cathie's family could be saved as a unit, but I couldn't see how it would ever be possible.

My Sources of Strength and Courage

Cathie felt abandoned by her parents. She was suffering greatly, and needed comfort. Once again, I talked to her about Jesus on the cross. Jesus asked his Father in heaven why He had abandoned Him. Of course, God did not actually abandon Jesus, but it seemed that way at the time. I pointed out that Jesus suffered even though He had done nothing wrong. I emphasized that she had done nothing wrong, either. She was not impressed. Nothing consoled her. She wanted her parents, period.

When I was single and teaching family religion in the homes of my students, I went on a trip to Europe. This trip was a pilgrimage to holy places, sponsored by a priest who also organized it. Wanting to become a better person and a more vibrant and informed teacher, I decided to open my heart to God's will for me. The main attractions were Rome in Italy, Lourdes in France, and Fatima in Portugal. For me, the pompous, authoritarian, controlling aspect I felt in Rome was negative. Even though I was chosen to go with one other person from the tour to obtain our group audience tickets with the Pope, I did not sense being in a holy place. God was not the center of all this, pride was. All I could think of, as I mounted the huge immaculately clean staircases and passed the Swiss Guards to the Vatican office for pilgrims, was how foreign all of this would have been to Jesus. Actually, I was embarrassed as a Christian. No matter how hard I tried to justify the ambiance of wealth for God, I couldn't.

Our family had always been poor. Our mother assured us that this was not important to God. Anyone who died with a history of caring about the needs of others and helping them would be greatly rewarded in heaven. This is what mattered in life. I wished that Rome was simpler in life style, and that the poor were better off because of it. Then I could be proud to be a Christian in Rome.

Lourdes and Fatima had all the spiritual qualities of loving, caring, and doing that I associated with church in my childhood. I loved them. Walking in the evening procession at Lourdes was absolutely unforgettable. The sweet song of "Ave, Ave, Ave Maria," with the endless line of candle-carrying pilgrims, was so faith-charged that my whole being was energized. Then the baths so prayerfully done in the Lourdes spring

71

water gave another powerful boost of positive caring. Everyone working there was a volunteer. No one was in it for the money. What an inspiration! At Fatima we prayed the rosary with such complete awe and respect that once again, I was spiritually empowered. This was my idea of Christianity. I could easily imagine Jesus walking among the people here.

Back in the States I internalized these experiences repeatedly by sharing them with the families I taught. I also shared them with my parents, brothers and sisters by the usual showing of slides and souvenirs.

Now, as we endured the karma of Cathie's family's neglect and abuse, we drew on all the spiritual strength from my family's faith, hope, and love. We went one day at a time and managed to keep going with our resolve to give Cathie her chance.

Tips For Adoptive Parents

↞ Time out for negative behavior and a hug after a quiet time does wonders. Always give a reason for punishment. This teaches simple logic.

↞ Read everything you can that speaks to you about the behavior you see daily. This helps keep expectations realistic.

Books, Music, and Websites

⇀ Bolles, Edmund Blair. The Penguin Adoption Handbook: A Guide to Creating Your New Family. New York: the Viking Press, 1984. One step at a time through the adoption process.

↞ Utah Parents.com—a free resource center for Utah Parents: http://www.utahparents.com/

Abandonment

Arriving back at my baby-sitter's, I found Cathie waiting anxiously for me. She wanted to know right away, "When me Mommy and Daddy come get me?" After hearing a five-hour description of horrible living conditions, I couldn't believe she wanted them back. When I explained it would be a while before they could take her back, she gave me her big lower lip pout. She turned away and held her clown doll for comfort. I told her they would probably visit her soon. This was March and I hoped they would comply with the check for lice and visit by April.

They did. And unknown to all of us, the April visit was their last. They didn't tell anyone they were leaving. When they failed to appear for their next visit, Jean explained to Cathie that her parents moved and didn't tell her where they went. Cathie refused to believe they had gone without her. Maybe Cathie needed a more clear and repeated explanation—I don't know. Her anxiety level was now at an all time high. Her head twitched.

After Cathie's parents did not return for her, she began acting out her understanding of abandonment. She was playing with her dolls one day in spring, and I could hear her from our kitchen window. She put her dolls in a car seat on the stoop and began to walk away saying, "Bye bye. I wove you and I'm never coming back."

Realizing what she was doing, I went out the front door and said, "Your other mommy and daddy did leave you, but we never will. They did not know how to take care of you because no one taught them. We know how."

She pointed at me and repeated the concept, "You know how to take care of me." Then she went quickly back to playing tenderly with her dolls. She understood once again. I needed to repeat this idea many times, and each time she listened as if it were the first.

Now I realized that the parental rights of Cathie's birth mother and father would be in jeopardy, and Cathie would become available for adoption. But I wondered how she would handle this, since she didn't believe it was true. Day by day, I learned my answer. One day, as she was watching "Little House on the Prairie" on TV, she commented about the fire she saw. "Me house burn. Mommy and Daddy die in fire," she said matter-of-factly.

Wondering what she was talking about, I questioned her: "Did you get burned in the fire too?"

"No. Me not there. Me here," she answered as if I had asked her a very stupid question.

I called Jean and told her what Cathie had said. Jean said this was very interesting to hear because many children come to the conclusion of parents dying in a fire if they don't see them for a long period of time. Jean said, "There probably isn't much you can say to Cathie except that her parents were not in a fire. She will have to gradually realize the truth of her abandonment. I really wish that the parents had said good-bye to their children.

It would have made life much easier for the children in the long run. "

"Really?" I questioned in disagreement. "It seems to me that this would be more heartbreaking for the children."

"No, it actually isn't," said Jean. "When the parents say good-bye, the children know what is going on. They know their parents are not blaming them for the separation. They also feel free to be adopted."

Not convinced, I hung up, glad that Cathie did not have to experience the heartbreak of having to say good-bye to her parents, as Jean had suggested. I didn't know how that could be better, since she still had the problem of no parents returning. Now, in retrospect, I agree with Jean. Cathie lost at least three years of carefree childhood joy because she didn't understand what had happened to her parents.

Cathie and Chris before Tommy joined our family

My Sources of Strength and Courage

Because of Cathie's constant sniffles, I was always looking for information on allergies and diets for good behavior. I purchased and used the following books:

Davis, Francyne. *The Low Blood Sugar Cookbook*. New York: Bantam Books Inc. 1973 revised in 1985.

Frazier, Claude A., M.D. *Parent's Guide To Allergy In Children*. New York: Double Day & Company Inc. 1973.

Fredericks, Carlton, Ph.D. *Low Blood Sugar and You*. New York:Perigee Book, 1985.

Tips For Adoptive Parents

✦ Pity is very detrimental, while empathy is necessary.
✦ Physically abused children often feel cold when others do not.

Tommy Joins Our Family

9

One day, Jean gave us a call to let us know that Tommy's foster parents were going on a vacation and needed a babysitter for him. She thought this would be a good time to see if he fit into our family. If he did, he could stay permanently. We welcomed the proposal. "Cathie, guess what? Your baby brother is coming to live with us!"

"Ommy come here wis me? He my baby! When he come?"

"He'll be here in a few days. What should we do to get ready for him?"

"Ge Ommy rib and bol. Ge pisure of him wis me."

She was more excited than I had ever seen her. She wanted him to have his own crib and bottle. Although she was only four years old and scarcely able to talk, she made plans as though she were his mother. We planned to get photographs at the local department store. She wanted him included right away. I was impressed with her foresight, and asked his foster parents if I could pick him up just for the portrait. We did this, and now have a treasured picture of the two of them that we might not have had without Cathie's request.

As I watched how happy Cathie was about her brother, I felt that we were fortunate to be able to get them together. She seemed to need to assure herself of a family. She played with her dolls saying, "This is my Mommy and Daddy. Tommy will stay here. I like this Mommy and Daddy and Tommy and Chris. Mommy and Daddy like Cathie and Tommy and Chris."

Tommy resembled Brian significantly. He was a towhead with curls and a constant smile, chubby with excess baby fat. Brian's baby pictures looked very similar, and we felt blessed to know he might become a member of our family.

Cathie's requested photo of herself and her baby brother.

Tommy arrived just as the sun was setting on a beautiful summer's day. His foster mother had dressed him for bed. He looked so cuddly in his nightie and big fuzzy bunny slippers. Cathie ran to him and hugged and kissed him. She had visited him many times and always asked to bring him with us. Now her wish had come true. Tommy was delighted with all the attention. Ten-month-old Chris was delighted with the presence of another child.

After giving us his clothes, schedule, and medical history, his foster mother gave him a sweet goodbye, being careful not to let him see her sorrow. She had foster-parented over a hundred babies and knew how to think only of the child's good. She and her kind husband had given Tommy gentle, loving care for seven months.

Tommy knew us from visits to his foster home. He came easily to Cathie and she took him by the hand as he shuffled in his bunny slippers around our home. She wanted to share her toys with him. He was so trusting and comfortable with her that it seemed he remembered her. I wondered if she would treat him the way we treated Chris, or the way she had seen her parents treat Tommy.

We prepared Tommy's crib in Chris's nursery. Since Tommy was just six months older than Chris, it was a little like having twins. They both went to bed easily the first week. Chris seemed happy to have Tommy in his room.

The next day, while Cathie went off to preschool and Brian to work, Chris and I played with Tommy. Brian made the children a large double play pen. Chris shared with Tommy nicely. Neither one could talk yet. I took turns swinging them in our indoor baby swing. Tommy was a sweet, silent child. Even so, tears would often come to his eyes, and he would look at me sadly. I held him and rocked him, wondering what it must be like to have a third set of parents in just sixteen months of life.

Tommy was such a cooperative, good boy that he almost fit in too easily. He even used the potty nicely. We had heard that children who seem to be dreams come true usually have big problems later. Surely, this wouldn't be true of beautiful little Tommy.

After a while I became aware that Cathie and Tommy both wanted our constant attention, and cried easily if they did not get it. When we ignored this behavior, Cathie cried louder or did something negative, like urinating wherever she was. Tommy would just stop crying and begin to play independently. Apparently Cathie was regressing a bit.

By the third day, Tommy was adjusting very well. But Cathie was so envious of all the attention he got that she announced, "Take Tommy backs."

"We can't," I answered. "Tommy's foster parents are away on vacation. He has to stay with us."

I smiled as she left to play. After a few days, most families would like to take a child back to wherever. But, thank heavens, they can't.

For the next two days we entertained my brother and his family, from out of state. They had their four children with them. We traveled to the mountains for sightseeing and picnics. It was fun, but exhausting. Tommy cried a lot. Chris was delighted with all of the attention from my brother's family. Cathie tried desperately to get as much attention as the babies, but failed. Finally, out of frustration, she blurted out, "Me pell me name, C-a-t-h-i-e."

"Oh Cathie, that's such a big girl," we all praised.

She had discovered that she could get attention by being big instead of little. I was elated with her creativity. She had solved her own problem.

When our company left, Cathie began to show me how she combined the different ways of treating Tommy. First she would be very sweet, and then abruptly cruel. To Tommy in his play pen she said, "Tommy is so good, s-o-o-o good. Is Tommy a good boy? Yes! No! No! Tommy is bad boy!" As Cathie said the word "bad" I heard her hit him. I ran in to talk to her about what she was doing.

"Tommy is a baby," I explained to her.

"Tommy is a baby. Babies are good. They are not bad," I explained to her.

She accepted this fact and I never heard her hit him again. However, when she played with her dolls, she treated them cruelly.

When Tommy's foster parents returned from vacation, his foster mother came to see him. He would not focus his eyes on her. Instead he would look past her and walk away as if she were not there. I asked her why he was doing this. She said it was because he wanted to stay with us. She was happy for him. Brian and I were a little mystified, but quietly pleased. Tommy would stay.

Chris enjoyed Tommy's presence and thrived. Several weeks later, Chris said his first word, hot. I had the oven on and he was holding on to the kitchen cupboards coming close to the stove. I stopped him and said, "hot." He repeated it. I was so thrilled that I called Brian and asked him if we could get a sound movie camera right away so that we could record the two babies' first words and months together. He agreed and we have these treasures forever.

Cathie was settling down now with Tommy, but she sometimes played too roughly with him. Once she swung him around by his arm and his head hit a door frame. The injury was not serious, but I sent her to her room.

She cried a short time and came to me saying, "When I grow up I'm going to take care of my kids, too. "

She was beginning to compare our parenting with that of her parents, and to know that ours was better. It was so rewarding to hear her express this. It made it all worth while.

Tommy turned his emotions on and off like a faucet. One minute he would be crying big crocodile tears over a *no* for something he wanted. The next he would be playing with a toy as if nothing had been said.

Cathie sometimes resented our corrections of her treatment of Tommy. She would be negative and grumpy. I sat down with her and explained that parents are supposed to tell their children how to behave. Then I reminded her about her own desire to be like us. She seemed overwhelmed. So I tried another approach. "When I was a little girl, Cathie, I had to do what my mother and father said. Now I am grown up and get to do things the way I want. When you grow up, you can too."

That was all she needed to know. She began to run errands willingly and to have a cooperative attitude. She was such a joy at this time.

"Me wearn A,B,C and wite name," she announced one day.

She wanted me to teach her. After watching me write letters and pay bills, she wanted to do the same. I began to teach her, and she learned to write her name immediately, but the A,B,C's took a long time.

Chris and Tommy began having problems sharing the same nursery. Chris cried excessively and Tommy became cross from lack of sleep. We had to separate them. Chris stayed in his nursery and Tommy moved to a room of his own, an easy solution. They both slept better.

Chris began to walk with more confidence and play more with Tommy. They both loved trucks. We laughed to hear Chris trying new words. He mixed *hot* with *truck* and called it a *huck*. Tommy still didn't talk. He babbled all the time but we could not distinguish any words.

We were told that children delay speech development if they experience trauma. So we weren't alarmed. Then, at the age of seventeen months, he parroted me as clear as a bell with the big word, *tractor*. I praised him for it with such joy that he quickly picked up on the fun of talking.

Brian and I had hoped to experience the joy of seeing children develop from stage to stage, and this was another hope being realized. How fortunate we felt. We were euphoric. Tommy was such a blessing for our family. However, we learned in one of our conferences for adoption that adoptive children who adapted easily in the beginning would be likely to have problems later. Tommy was so beautiful and precious we just hoped for the best, as all parents do.

Tommy in the peach tree, loving this attention.

86

When Tommy was three years old, I realized that he fell down a lot. He had very poor muscle tone, and it seemed that all he wanted to do was eat. So I devised a schedule of exercise to overcome these problems: each night, after supper, I had him go up and down our basement stairs ten times. Then, when he could, he copied Brian doing push-ups and sit-ups. He loved the attention and it worked. He lost weight, gained muscle tone, and stopped falling down so much. His teachers noticed his progress and were surprised. Tommy was very proud of his accomplishments. These exercises took place for several years from pre-school on into the elementary years.

My Sources of Strength and Courage

The joy and satisfaction of adding Tommy to our family were so gratifying that Brian and I basked in them for days. The positive value of joy is priceless. I allowed this joy to permeate my whole self each morning during meditation. Zen meditation has the wonderful capability of freezing any treasured memory forever. Then later, when this source of strength is needed, it can be brought back with clarity. I used this practice frequently at this time.

Knowing that this would be an emotionally volatile time in our lives, I carefully stored each life-fulfilling moment of joy, contentment, and satisfaction as a "frozen gift from God" for later use in my Zen memory bank. Just as my mother canned vegetables and fruits for winter survival, so I froze my spiritual stash for the possible uniting of a unique family.

When I was learning how to do Zen meditation, I read a book called *Zen and the Art Of Motorcycle Maintenance*. It was this strange little book that gave me insight into this method of calling forth inner strength. This is how I would do it: At the time of awareness, taking a deep breath, I repeated my regular mantra: "I am Veronica. I am breathing. Thank you, God, for this joy." With a few silent breaths, the awareness was frozen in my memory. I still do this on a regular basis. I freeze scenes of beauty in my memory so that I will be able to recall them when I can no longer hike or travel. Each time I recall these positive memos I experience the same peace and lightheartedness I felt at the time of the original awareness. This not only makes me feel strong spiritually, it also makes me feel better physically.

Tips For Adoptive Parents

✦ With professional guidance, ourselves, we can be our child's best therapists.

✦ We should never underestimate a child's ability to accept past suffering. They need to be helped over one trauma at a time.

Books, Music, and Websites

— Eitz, Maria. *Dark Rice*. Waukesha, Wisconsin : Country Beautiful Publishing, 1975. This is the story of a Vietnamese orphan. I met the author and was much inspired by her person as well as her story.

— Taylor, Rosemary. *Turn My Eyes Away*. Boulder, Colorado: Friend For All Children, 1976. This is an unforgettable book about children in Vietnam from 1967 to 1975. Chris loved to look at the pictures in this book. I was inspired by the complete dedication of the people who cared for these children.

❧ Resources for Foster Parenting and Adoption—if you are unfamiliar with the local programs or agencies working with maltreated children in your area, this site can often help you get directed to local programs:
http://www.bcm.tmc.edu/civitas/info_foster_adoption.htm

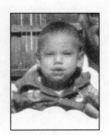

Joys and Heartaches For Chris

While Cathie was angry about her parents not returning, Chris was content. Babies bond with their caretakers, and his mother had visited with him so seldom that he knew Brian and me as his parents. I often wished that she would make up her mind about her own life so that Chris could get on with his. What did she want her life to be now? She was still trying to decide what kind of life partner she wanted.

Shortly after Chris's birth she had again gotten pregnant. This time her baby's father was a gentle person. For a while she moved out of our county to live with her sister, and was no longer eligible for visits with Chris. Later she moved back, and seemed to settle down, inviting the expected baby's father to move in with her.

Since her other four children were in the custody of their father, she wanted to make a new start. Now she believed that she could take Chris back and care for him properly. After reviewing her case, the judge decided that she should wait until her new baby was born to see how well she met its needs.

After the judge's decision, she didn't bother to see Chris for over two and a half months. This time proved to be very happy for Chris. He learned to walk and talk, both of which he did with lots of enthusiasm. We could tell that he was very bright.

Not wanting these precious moments to be forgotten, Brian and I did the same thing millions of other parents have done: we purchased cameras. One was for still pictures, and the other for movies. We had great fun with these all through the summer as we hiked in the mountains and enjoyed fishing.

At the beginning of the summer, Brian and I felt the need to get away for a vacation. We decided to see the Black Hills of South Dakota. We asked some foster parent friends to baby-sit for Chris. Cathie was happy to stay with one of Brian's sisters. It proved to be good for us, but not for the children. We were gone for five days. Chris became feverish and had ear infections. When we returned he didn't know us at first, which was hard for us. His babysitters, who were foster parents who had experienced this many times, reassured us he would soon remember.

After picking up Chris, we went home and waited for Brian's sister to bring Cathie back from her farm, about a half-hour from us. We welcomed Cathie and were confused with her reaction to seeing us. She fell on the floor, kicking and crying. I later discovered that Cathie had fully expected to see her birth parents. We had been calling ourselves "Mommy and Daddy" to her, so naturally our relatives and friends did, also. When Brian's sister told Cathie that her mommy and daddy were back from vacation, she thought only of her birth parents.

We were settling back into the routine of foster-parenting when we got a phone call from Chris's caseworker, Carla.

"Hello, Mrs. Brunner. Did you enjoy your vacation?" she asked in a very pleasant tone.

"Yes. How have you been?" I reluctantly asked. This had to be trouble.

"I've been great. I am calling to inform you that I will be transferring Chris to a different caseworker. I hope that

91

everything works out for him and his mother. She is really having a hard time trying to get her life together. It has been a long
time since I placed Chris with you. It will be up to his new caseworker now. She will be calling you this week. Good luck!"

When I hung up I didn't know what to think. Carla sounded as if she felt that Chris's case needed to be terminated
because of the time he had spent in foster care. That would
mean that he would have a chance of being free for adoption.
Now, we had to wait and see what his new caseworker thought.

A few days later we met Carla's replacement, "Exasperella,"
who believed firmly that birth parents were best for raising a
child. I think you can tell from the name I chose for her that I
did not agree with the decisions she made for Chris. She
informed us that she would be visiting Chris to get to know
him. This was fine, and the visit was memorable for me because
she was very impressed with Chris's laughter. Her comment
was, "He is such a funny baby."

"Exasperella" explained her plan to prepare Chris for a permanent reunion with his own family, starting with weekly
supervised visits. These visits would become longer and more
frequent until Chris was as comfortable with his family as he
was with us. Then he would begin to stay overnight. Eventually
his time with us would be shorter than his time with them.

Although this sounded great in theory, Brian and I sensed
that it meant a lot of emotional trauma for Chris. Knowing how
much Cathie and her siblings were suffering from similar emotional upheavals, we hated the thought of it happening to Chris.
He was developing with good happy strides. I was so upset
about it that I found myself crying easily. Brian tried to console
me by assuring me that Chris would make it. Although Brian

said this, he began tossing and turning at night, and was as worried as I.

Our instincts told us to fight for Chris's right to his own happiness. His mother was not able to assure the judge that she wouldn't hurt Chris, so Brian and I were also concerned about his safety. After one of his visits with his mother he returned to us with his diaper containing cigarette burns on the inside. I was alarmed, but not experienced enough with the court system to know that I should immediately call a neighbor to witness the burns on his soiled diaper. Instead, I washed out the soil and then took it to our lawyer. She explained my mistake and told me what to look for in the future.

While the majority of Social Service's personnel are warm, caring, and highly professional, a few aren't. Unfortunately, Chris's new caseworker was one of the few. When we inquired about how much therapy Chris's mother had received, "Exasperella" became defensive, reminding us that we were not Chris's birth parents. She didn't understand how much we loved him. She admitted that his mother had been given a psychological interview, not therapy, and suggested we talk to the psychologist for reassurance.

I accepted this offer, hoping that I could plead Chris's case with someone who better understood trauma and children. Instead I met with a man who did not like having his decision challenged. Fortunately, I had been accompanied on this visit to the psychiatrist by Mary, Chris's mother's volunteer helper, whose support was sorely needed when the doctor told me that he believed that I, not Chris's mother, had put the cigarette burns on Chris's diaper.

Brian and I now decided to hire a lawyer to defend Chris's rights. The lawyer encouraged us to write a letter to the judge. I did this, informing him of every detail of Chris's abuse, neglect, and allergy to dairy products. The net result of all our concern was that the judge ordered a list of requirements that had to be met by Chris's mother in order for her to keep him permanently. This helped allay some of our anxiety.

It was upsetting to know that Chris's Guardian Ad Litem had never met him. I insisted that he come to our home and meet Chris and me. He explained to me that he could do nothing to change the outcome of Chris's situation. It was his job to try to protect Chris if he was in obvious danger, and nothing I said about Chris's mother seemed to be all that dangerous. He said that children have to go back to parents if they show any improvement, and since this was the case, Chris would go back to his mother.

Christmas was near and the judge said Chris had to be placed with his mother before Christmas. Her other baby had been born and she was caring for it with no trouble. The new baby's father had moved in with them and no violence had been reported. Although Chris spent considerable time with his mother, he never went for a visit without crying. Brian and I thought this was a "no go" for the return. We felt that Chris would feel abandoned if the plan were carried out too soon.

If Chris enjoyed his visits and seemed eager to return to his mother, we would have felt better. As it was, we had to prepare him for a final separation from us when he still thought that we were his parents. "Exasperella" had told us that according to the latest thinking, babies could understand more than we thought. She suggested that we tell him what was happening and hope for the best. So, I talked to Chris almost as if he were an adult. I told him, "If she hurts you, scream and cry. Don't stop until you get help."

Foster parenting has its ups and downs. This was a most painful down. But at least we had given Chris a very happy and healthy first year. All of our friends and relatives supported us with their prayers and best wishes.

Another igloo attempt in the backyard

On the morning Chris was leaving, I prepared two boxes of portraits, clothing, and toys for him and his mother. In case his mother might not be able to care properly for him, I kept a few special toys so he would have familiar playthings waiting for him if he returned to us. I watched Chris play with abandon, wondering if I would ever see or hear of him again. I was worried for his safety and angry that the judge had so much power over his life without ever sharing in it at all. I fervently prayed that what was about to happen to him would not destroy the happy, joyful little boy that we loved so much.

Chris was supposed to be picked up by a driver working for Social Services. The same driver took him to his many visits. She was late returning from a party, and Brian and I were very grateful because it gave Brian time to get home from work to say good-bye, along with Cathie and me. We were in agony as Chris was placed, crying and screaming, into the car for his trip to his mother's apartment. He could tell that something was different. All of his things were going with him. We were so sad.

We kissed him and smiled the best we could, because we did not want him to feel our pain. Cathie watched us in wonderment. As Chris was driven away, still crying at the top of his lungs, Brian and I clung to each other and openly sobbed. This was the most horrible day of our lives. Cathie did not know what to do. I asked her if she was sad that Chris was gone and not coming back.

"Chris not coming back. Me sad. Me not cry."

"That's okay," I assured her with a hug.

She pulled coldly away from my grasp and went to hold her doll in a pensive silence. I wondered if she thought she might be the next to go to a different home. Maybe she was frustrated that Chris could go back to his mother, but she couldn't go back to hers.

Now began our long ordeal with temper tantrums. Nothing satisfied her. If I suggested that we go to the park for a picnic, she stomped down the basement stairs to her room and slammed her door. No matter how much I tried to be positive about something for her to do, she responded with "No!"

Although these tantrums were her first for us, they were incredibly frequent. She had one almost every time I spoke to her. Neither her therapist nor I could lessen her emotional pain at this time. She became a five-year-old hellion. I didn't want to focus on her problems too much, because I noticed they then got worse.

One day, as I was preoccupied and thinking, Cathie came up from behind me and hugged me, saying, "Mommy need help. Me help." I was taken completely by surprise by her new ability to empathize, and I hugged her and said, "Thank you." Her hug was so comforting. I didn't know a child could make a parent feel so good. Waiting to hear about Chris was easier now.

During our fourteen weeks of preparing to help Chris return to his birth mother, Tommy became more outgoing. As he spent more time alone with me, he became quite affectionate. He laughed big belly laughs quite often. I made a mental note that if Chris did come back to our family, I would need to make special time for Tommy.

On the day of Chris's departure from our family, Tommy was taking his usual nap. He missed the good-bye, but noticed that Chris was gone. About a week after Chris left, Tommy said, "Chris, Chris."

"Chris went bye-bye," I said. "He is not coming back." Tommy never called his name again, so maybe he understood.

Laughter was constant for him now. He was basking in all the attention that was being showered on him. But I felt empty, wondering if Chris was getting equal attention from his mother. I couldn't help feeling resentment and frustration that Tommy and Cathie could have our loving care, while Chris might be in danger for his life.

My Sources of Strength and Courage

This period of waiting to hear about Chris's welfare was a big test for me. I felt as if my faith, learned early from my mother, was being challenged. Each morning when I awoke, my first thought was of Chris's safety. I prayed for his Guardian Angel to watch over him and inspire his mother to do the right thing. Then I could get my cup of coffee and begin my meditation.

Each Sunday, as we went to church without Chris, our friends sympathized with our pain and encouraged us with their hope and prayers. The strength we received from our church community cannot be exaggerated. It, along with our families' support, sustained us as we inched through our agony.

Brian had his work to go to each day and I was busy with family chores. But when the work stopped for us, the wondering about Chris began. Now I understood my mother's pain when my brothers had to go to the Korean War. We saw her massaging her arms because they were numb from fear. I felt numb all over when I feared for Chris's life.

This reminded me about an episode of spiritual growth in my father's life that all of our family at home witnessed. Each night we had the bedtime ritual of saying the rosary and a few other prayers. My mother led the prayers in the dark room, with only a single candle burning between statues of Jesus, Mary, and Joseph. Our father did not participate. He sat in the kitchen next to where we prayed and listened to the news on the radio, which he turned down. As we stared at the statues and repeated the prayers, we calmed down from whatever the day had brought. It was so peaceful for me; it seemed that heaven might be something like this. Then, without any warning, one night my mother called to my father, "Dad, if you ever want to see your boys alive again, get in here and pray for them."

I can still see the outline of my father's tall form coming through the doorway, and him humbly kneeling beside a chair to join the rest of the family in praying the rosary. From that night on he prayed the rosary every night with us, and all of my brothers returned safely home.

Remembering this, I fully expected Chris to be protected also. For me, faith was a crucial part of family life. After waiting so long to have some kind of a family, this just had to be accepted as a part of it.

Adding Tommy to our family was a help for me when Chris had to leave. Those months of joy all built up the strength to endure our loss of Chris. The strength of friends, family and church, combined with personal faith and meditation, made it possible to accept our pain.

Tips For Adoptive Parents

  ↞ If possible, analyze the thought process after a temper tantrum. Cathie received help through therapy with child meditation.
  ↞ Small children usually need to be accompanied to psychotherapy.

Books, Music, and Websites

  — Spencer, Penny K., Publisher. *The National Directory of Children, Youth & Families Services, 1999-2000.* Englewood, Colorado, 1999. Help for any family need.
  ❧ Baby Bag® Online—"The In-Site to Parenting." http://www.babybag.com/

Chris Comes Home

11

I expressed my frustration and worry to my friends at church.
They suggested that we hire a private detective to watch out
for his safety. They even offered to help pay the detective if the
amount became exorbitant. Brian and I decided to do this.

It was quite a relief to be doing something for Chris. We
were very anxious to know how he was, but we received very
little information because the detectives were rarely able to see
Chris with his mother. They informed us that from outside the
house they could hear a baby crying in another room. Later
they didn't even hear him anymore.

I was alarmed, wondering if she had done something crimi-
nal. So I called "Exasperella" to see if she could tell me anything
about Chris. She informed me that he was no longer with his
mother by her own request, as she could not endure his crying
and squealing. His mother had called Social Services and asked
them to come and get him before she hurt him. His mother even
said that someone who could make him happy could adopt him.

"I took him to another foster family for long-term placement until he can be adopted, " she informed me quite matter-
of-factly.

I had mixed feelings of relief and disbelief. Chris was no
longer in danger of his life, but why didn't "Exasperella" bring

him back to us? Why did she place him with a family of strangers? Didn't she tell us how important it was to gradually introduce him to another family? Why was she ignoring her own advice? I knew Chris must be feeling completely abandoned.

Brian had been waiting to hear about Chris, so I called him and we shared our relief and incredulity. Chris had only stayed with his mother for three weeks and five days, and for now we reveled in joy for his safety. We were confident that this placement had to be a mistake and that he would be coming back home soon.

Wondering what to do next, I called some friends at Social Services. They were not all in agreement as to what we could expect. Some were surprised that we expected to have Chris returned to our family, since "Exasperella" had already placed him with another family. Some were appalled at what was happening to Chris. We were completely stunned! It seemed to us that not returning Chris to our home soon was very cruel to him. Surely he must be greatly disturbed by these changes in caregivers. None of this was making any sense to us. Why wasn't he given back to us? We were, after all, the only family he had known.

When we asked these questions, we were given a list of reasons that all added up to one fact: we loved Chris too much. How could this be? When we spoke with other foster parents we found that our experience with Chris was the norm rather than the exception, but we refused to let him suffer from this bureaucratic nonsense.

After stewing over the situation for a week, we decided to confront "Exasperella" and see if she understood Chris's predicament. She didn't. Furthermore, she couldn't understand why we cared about him at all. She thought that we would be happy for him and go on with our lives.

We contacted the Social Service personnel who trained us for foster care and found that they did understand our frustration with Chris's placement. They advised "Exasperella" to come up with a solution that was considerate of Chris's emotional needs. Under this advisement "Exasperella" informed us of his whereabouts and agreed that we could call the foster home for a visit. I felt hurt, humiliated, and confused, but we were so happy to be able to see him that we overlooked the pain and made plans for the visit.

Chris's new foster home was ten miles away. On the long ride there my heart was singing. No matter what it took, I was determined to get Chris back into our family. I couldn't stand the thought of him being abandoned the way Cathie and Tommy had been.

When we arrived, we were greeted by at least six children. Chris was in the crowd. Brian spotted him quickly. He had changed so much that at first I didn't recognize him. The children welcomed us and said that their parents would be back from the grocery store soon.

"Hi, Chris!" I blurted out as I approached and picked him up to hold in my arms. What a relief! He really was safe! He just looked at me for a moment with a questioning expression. So I began talking in baby babble that he used to say with me. Then he recognized me and became angry. He hit me on my cheek several times.

Cathie's psychiatrist had warned me that this might happen. She said that Chris would blame us for his confusion and strike out at us. She said that it is the same "blame" many pet owners experience when they return from vacations.

"Are you angry, Chris?" I asked him, understanding his emotion. He looked at me with affection and clung to me. He never hit me again.

Handing Chris to Brian, we shared our elation at being able to embrace him. Chris was smiling now. His foster family was a large one consisting of mostly foster children. After his new foster parents returned home, we exchanged ideas about where to go from there. Since "Exasperella" was not moving on this, we would have to do it, ourselves. We decided that we would take Chris home during the week and return him for weekends. In the meantime we would have to negotiate with "Exasperella." This took five painful weeks.

Brian had a hard time believing that "Exasperella" could have a college degree and still understand so little about children and parenting. We had to be tested by a psychologist at our own expense to see if we had the necessary skills to parent Chris. We also had to take Chris to this same psychologist to see if he had bonded with us. We all came through with flying colors. Chris considered us his parents, and Brian and I tested in the ninety-eighth percentile. These test results were sent to us and to the Social Service supervisor, and "Exasperella" had to admit she made a mistake. Finally, one evening, she called and said that we could become Chris's foster parents again—this time with the option to adopt.

We were ecstatic! At last Chris was our baby to love and cherish always. When we went to her office the next day, the main supervisor went with us. We wondered how "Exasperella" would handle this loss of face. She was wearing blue jeans and sitting with her legs crossed under her. She silently pointed to chairs for the three of us. The supervisor frowned in disapproval of such unprofessional behavior. She told us our test results and said she was closing his case. She planned to leave the department, go back to school, and perhaps become a judge. That was how she saved face. She then uncrossed her legs and rose as a cue for us to leave. We walked out in disgusted silence.

Once we were out of her office we spoke freely to the supervisor, thanking her for her support and concern for Chris's welfare. She wished us well and sent us on our way to pick up Chris. When we arrived to get him his foster mother had packed his clothes. Chris knew what this meant. As we thanked her and visited a while, Chris kept running to the door, and pointing to our van saying, "Go, go."

Chris was right. We needed to put an end to confusion about which home and family were his. Chris's foster child traumas had finally ended at the age of seventeen months. Chris, Cathie, Tommy, Brian and I all went to Arby's to celebrate. Now we had our family.

My Sources of Strength and Courage

Focusing on the negative qualities of Chris's caseworker was not healthy for our family. Brian began looking for the humor in our lives, which was a great idea. I laughed at his funny stories from work or the newspaper. We lightened up our spirits and the children began to relax. They were not fighting and crying to have their way so much.

We were glad to know one or two unprofessional caseworkers were not able to sway the entire system of our county's Social Services. But insensitive people were able to do a lot of damage. I could see that Chris had lost his basic trust in us. He frowned a lot and seldom laughed. I prayed daily for God to give Chris the inspiration needed to overcome these negative forces. He was so young. How long would it take before we could explain to him?

Brian and I had helped Chris become a member of our family again through our willingness to cooperate with the personnel at Social Services who were functioning on a professional level. This took a lot of humility and patience. We felt like saying nothing and hoping for the best, but our consciences would not allow it. Chris was suffering, and we were the ones who knew it and could correct the problem for him. If Social Services had not responded when they did, I was preparing to take his story to our local TV news troubleshooter. The supervisor told me she sensed this possibility and wanted to avoid it.

There are times when we need to look to our saintly heroes for examples of what to do. I was thinking of Saint Paul in Biblical times as I planned to expose Chris's case. I'm glad the supervisor guessed my resolve before I carried it out. I believe it helps our spiritual growth to have special heroes. As a high school student I used my free time to read about the lives of saints. After reading dozens of books, I remember choosing my two favorites, Saint Therese of Liseaux and Saint Aloysius Gonzaga. They both dedicated their lives to God at very young ages, and I wanted to be like them. For at least fifteen years I strove to emulate their perfection.

Now I know that no one is ever perfect, but I was able to be a more generous person because of this effort. I could endure suffering with more patience because of these virtuous aspirations in my youth. It was important to have these goals and to strive for them. As I matured, I learned it was not possible to be perfect and that this didn't matter. It was necessary only to be sincerely good. I relaxed and opened my mind to the karma of life.

Tips For Adoptive Parents

✦ Hiring an investigator is easier than you may imagine. We felt much better once we did. Our investigator was fair and specific, and admired our love for a foster child.

✦ Often, children understand without being able to verbalize. We were encouraged to explain what was happening no matter what we thought they could understand.

Books, Music, and Websites

⌐ Paulus, Trina. *Hope For the Flowers*. New York : Newman Press 1972. This is a tale about life and hope for children and adults.

⌐ Hall, Brian. *The Wizard of Maldoone*. New York: Paulist Press 1975. This book was written to help children and adults find their own dragons within themselves so they could discover personal peace.

⋈ Novagene's Web Oasis—foster parenting resources. The toughest job you'll ever love: http://www.novagene.com/fosterparenting_resources.html

Changing Cathie's Name

Cathie's name change took place in the fall before Chris went back to his birth mother. Many adoptive parents dream of giving their child a particular name when they adopt—the naming helps them feel a special bonding. I understood and accepted this, but had no intention of changing Cathie's name . . . until it became a matter of her safety.

No one had heard anything from Cathie and Tommy's birth parents for six months. They had disappeared, just as Jean had feared they would. When Social Services offered help, they refused and left. They had abandoned their children in this manner now for the fourth time. I overheard their father saying to their mother in the courtroom the day of their hearing, in a determined and defiant tone, "We'll have some more kids and this time they won't get them."

The big thing that bothered Cathie, of course, was the fact that her parents did not return. Her therapist informed me that she was beginning to forget what her mother looked like and she was frightened. Everywhere we went she looked at any woman passing by and said, "Are you my mother?" The woman would look at me in alarm, and I quickly explained that Cathie was a foster child who missed her mother.

As Halloween approached I explained to Cathie about "trick-or-treat." She loved the idea, just as most kids do. I found a darling mouse costume that she liked. Chris and Tommy were too small to understand any of the traditions, but, just as thousands of other parents do, Brian and I put them in costumes and drove them around to our relatives and friends. Once they received their first candy they wanted to come home and start eating. It was such great fun for us parents that we kept going until they fell asleep in the car.

"Is our little mousie ready for bed now?" I affectionately asked Cathie.

"Me cute wittle mousie," she said with satisfaction. "Me no more Cathie. Me Mousie now. You call me Mousie," she demanded.

"You want to be called Mousie all the time?" I queried. "Why?"

"Can't say name right," she replied. "People say, 'What you name?' Me say name, and nobody know me name."

She was right. Every time she tried to tell someone her name I would have to clarify it due to her poor enunciation.

It seemed like a harmless idea, so I went along with it for a short time. But calling her Mousie seemed too degrading, and I wondered if we should seriously think of another name for her.

Then we received an alarming phone call from Cathie and Tommy's caseworker, Jean. She had located their parents. They had gone to relatives with a plea to help them get their children back. Tommy and Cathie's aunts and uncles contacted Social Services and were willing to take care of the children. Jean was worried that this was only a ploy for eventually getting the children back to their abusive and neglectful parents.

She further warned us that the parents had threatened to kidnap them. Now the situation was critical!

We were not concerned about Cathie being kidnapped from our home, since their parents had no idea of our whereabouts, but we knew that they had been told in court where she went to preschool. It would be possible for them to go to the school and ask for her. She might recognize them and go with them. Now the name change looked necessary for her safety. We asked Jean if we could change her name. She gave it some thought and agreed that it might save her life.

"Cathie, would you like to have a pretty new name?" I asked as if it were just a fun thing to do.

"Me want new name. Es, es, es," she excitedly responded.

What fun! Brian, Cathie, and I began going through the baby book of names. This was almost better than naming a baby, because we already knew her personality. Now we just needed to match it with the appropriate name. We also wanted her to like her name. That was the difficult part. When we found a name that we both liked we asked her if she liked it, too. She did and we agreed to change her name to Mary.

We called Jean and her preschool, and all agreed that her name would be Mary. Of course we explained the reason for the change to her teachers so that they would know to call the police if anyone asked for her by the other name. Jean had already notified the police about the threat of kidnapping, and even remembered what the parents' vehicle looked like. It was an old white van with some dents in it. One day as I went to pick up Mary, I saw a vehicle matching this description. The police were cruising the area. The vehicle left and I never saw it again. Hoping that they had not tried to retrieve Mary, I anxiously went in to get her. Although she gave me the usual disappointed look of "not my mommie," I was enormously relieved to know that she was safe. We went home talking about school as we always did.

One day, shortly after the name change, Mary said, "All other kids at school want new names, too." Her teachers, Brian, and I had a good laugh.

"See how lucky you are, Mary? You are the only one who gets to have the name you want."

Mary has always been happy about the change. Her older brother, Steve, didn't like it one bit until we explained why, and then he accepted it. Tommy and Chris were still just learning to talk, so they were able to make the change with ease. We are grateful that it all went so smoothly and she is still unknown to her parents.

Tips For Adoptive Parents

✦ A schedule is of supreme importance to a child. It may be the only control s/he has over knowing what to expect.

✦ Do not expect youthful babysitters to understand abused and neglected children. Try to get adult sitters.

Books, Music, and Websites

– Greenfield, Eloise. *Me and Neesie*. New York: Harper, Thomas Y. Crowell Company, 1975. This helped our children understand how special everyone is.

❧ Univ of MN Parenting Education Resources—INFO-U is a free public service of the University of Minnesota Extension Service. Parenting information factsheets are available on-line. This same information is also available via telephone messages and fax: http://www.parenting.umn.edu/

Family Celebrations

13

Most childless couples dream of happy family holidays and birthdays. Our first ones with Chris were exciting for us, but Chris was too young to know what a holiday was. We took lots of pictures for his own memories. My parents flew out to share Christmas with us and see baby Chris. It was a very happy time for all of us, and we still have those great pictures.

Even though we were going through considerable trauma preparing for Chris to return to his mother for the second fall and winter, we had a warm, memorable Thanksgiving and a great birthday party for Mary. As I purchased the traditional turkey dinner groceries, Mary talked about each item. Apparently she had never experienced Thanksgiving before. She had never heard of turkey, or cranberries, or yams. But she was eager to enjoy a special day, and this holiday would be one to always treasure with all five of us together. It proved to be so satisfying that we were unprepared for our next three Christmases.

Shortly after this first Thanksgiving with Mary and Tommy, Jean called to update us on court proceedings for them. She had been concerned that their parents might show up in court and request that custody be given to their father's sister. This aunt had once called and asked if she could have custody of the children, but to our great relief, Jean had recently spoken with her by phone and she was no longer asking for custody. Aware that their parents continued drinking and fighting, she realized that the children were better off with other parents.

The court date for the termination of parental rights due to abandonment was set for just two days before Christmas. I marked my calendar and never dreamed that four-year-old Mary was aware of what might take place, but she became grumpy and negative, much like a sick child. I thought she just wanted to see her parents and could not express herself, and feeling frustrated with her lack of cooperation I tried to get her into what I thought of as the Christmas spirit. This was a gross misunderstanding of her pain.

Our three children enjoying a celebration.

Fortunately, Mary's fifth birthday was coming up before Christmas. Not knowing for sure what would happen in court, we decided to give her a big party. This helped to cheer her. She was happy to help make her own invitations. We invited her brother, Steve, and sister, Jenny, and many of our large family, and we got out the best china and crystal. What a great time she had! She was showered with gifts—receiving dolls, beautiful clothes and books, and, most of all, attention.

I had practiced with Mary (very much like a rehearsal for a play) the day before the party so that she would know what to expect and how she should act. Amazingly, she had an impeccable day. All of her worries were forgotten and she seemed like a well-groomed little princess for one day. We took many pictures, including a movie, and later on she asked to see the movie over and over. What a joy she could be! For many weeks she sang "Happy Birthday, dear Mary. Happy Birthday to me!"

Several days after her party we put up the Christmas tree. She was tense. Instead of being cooperative, she refused to help with any of the decorating. I wondered if this was another new experience, like Thanksgiving. Then I remembered that she had been taken from her parents at Christmas time the previous year. Her association with the tree was this awful anxiety. What could I do?

When I mentioned this problem to other foster parents they responded with the fact that many foster children are in this predicament. Christmas is not a happy memory for them. It takes several good Christmases to help these children enjoy the season. It was a difficult pill for me to swallow. To me all children had to enjoy Christmas as a time of being doted on, just because they were children.

118

Resentment toward her parents welled up within me because they had deprived me of this. The next two Christmases were equally bad. Although we put up the tree and opened presents, Mary would scream and cry and run to her room where she repeated loudly, "All mine fault." She was not at all interested in any of her toys or other Christmas gifts.

By the third Christmas it dawned on me what she meant. She thought that all of the events that led to her parents not returning were somehow her responsibility. Once I explained that her parents were to blame because they were adults, she was noticeably relieved. From that time on Christmases got better.

Tommy did not have these problems with Christmas. Although his first one was in a hospital recovering from a skull fracture, he showed only glee with all the gifts and decorations and sweet foods. He was a very happy toddler, and we doted on him with great pleasure.

Three days before Christmas the court was in session for the termination of Tommy and Mary's parents' rights. According to Jean, no parents or relatives showed up and the case was finalized. Coincidentally, the regular judge for that day was absent, and replaced by the same judge who had terminated the rights of these same parents nine years previously in the next county. There had been four children at that previous time also. The judge was incredulous at the pattern of neglect and abuse that this couple was repeating. He said he hoped they would never have any more children to abuse.

When Jean called to inform us that the termination had in fact taken place, I was relieved and happy to be assured that Mary and Tommy would become our family.

Not Mary! She asked me what Jean had said. When I cheerfully and excitedly explained that her parents would never be able to hurt her any more she began to cry. As I reached out to hold her, she pulled back and said, "Me want them to come and get me. Me wove them." She went into our family room and hugged her doll.

Several days after Christmas, Jean came to tell Mary that her parents couldn't be found and that we would be adopting her. I know now that she did not understand that conversation. She continued to wait for her parents to come for her. When they did not, she became more and more of a problem child. Each morning she sat in her bed and wet it, and sometimes she defecated. She sat with her bare bottom on her bed to soil it.

Even after Chris came back and our emotions were no longer on a roller coaster, Mary, now six years old, seemed to experience no end of turmoil. About every ten minutes she slammed doors, started crying, or stomped up or down the basement stairs. We had just had another bad Christmas and adoption was only a month away. We could not comfort her. In desperation and exhaustion, I wondered if adoption would be a mistake for her and us. Maybe another family would be able to meet her needs.

I asked her, "Mary, do you want us to adopt you or would you rather have someone else be your parents?"

"Stay with you," she answered firmly.

"Then you have to stop screaming and falling on the floor every time you don't like what is happening," I bargained.

She agreed, and gradually overcame her intense rage with her parents. Now I knew what Jean had meant when she said that it would have been better if their parents had said goodbye to them. It would have freed the children.

Finally, we decided that we would adopt all three children. With the help of other adoptive parents, we did all the paperwork ourselves and saved attorney's fees. Mary was six, and Tommy and Chris were two years old. We took them all along to court. Tommy and Chris were so young that we had to bribe them with a trip to McDonald's if they could sit quietly until the questions were all answered and the judge declared us their legal parents.

Chris's paper work had been delayed for months because three different men were his possible fathers. An ad in the paper gave each one his legal chance to protest the adoption. No one came forward, and the adoption was carried out. No one could take him away again.

Adoption day, 1982.

After the proceedings we took pictures with the judge. Mary wanted me to hold her because Brian was holding Tommy and Chris. When I picked her up, her whole body went limp like a rag doll. Chris and Tommy were too young to understand what was happening, but I had explained to Mary that we were her new family. She didn't seem to know if she was happy or not. We stopped at Brian's brother and sister-in-law's home to share our joy with them, and it was obvious to me that the children had no idea what the celebration was about. On the way home Mary sang a song about a "Blue Bird on my shoulder." I thought maybe she felt some joy.

Mary had lost her parents, and she really wasn't ready yet to have them replaced. We did not know this until later. All of the negative behavior that she could muster came out for two more years. Then once again I asked her, "Mary, do you want to go to a different home to live?"

"Yes," she honestly answered.

My heart sank like a stone because I knew that not all adoptions were successful, but I also felt relief because at least we were breaking the stalemate of endless rage. We were getting somewhere.

And yet, she was adopted. We were very bonded to her. How could we help her to bond with us?

I sensed that she thought she knew where she wanted to go. So, I carefully thought out my next question. "Who do you think will be in your new home?"

"My other mommy and daddy who weaved me here," she answered in a tone of voice that said I ought to know.

"Mary, if we took you to every house in this town, they would not be there," I explained. "Jean has looked everywhere for them. She can't find them. And neither can anybody else."

A light bulb went on and we were both very relieved. She smiled a special smile that has been a part of her personality ever since. When I explained to Brian what had just happened, he couldn't believe it.

Each Sunday I had what I called "Home Church" for the children. They took turns choosing the songs and bible stories for the service. After the service they all worked in their own Bible story workbooks. After the activity, I would hug Chris and Tommy because they sought physical affection, but Mary would always stand aloof and sad with her head down and her bottom lip out. She looked as if she wanted to be included. Many times before she had refused hugs—maybe she was ready now.

"Mary, we have been trying to love you, too, but you won't let us. It's up to you." I held out my arms, inviting her to come for a hug. Instead of accepting my offer, she turned and went sadly to her room.

After pouting and thinking for a half-hour, Cathy made her conscious transfer of love from her first family to ours. She came out of her bedroom and walked into the kitchen where Brian was making breakfast. Chris and Tommy were in the dining room with me, at the end of the kitchen. We could all see Mary as she announced clearly, "Mom, I've decided to love you. I'm going to love this whole family." And she meant it.

Once more I opened my arms, and this time she accepted with warm satisfaction. She had made her own decision with firm resolution like an adult. Yet she was an eight-year-old child who needed to experience childhood with security and unconditional love. That was when our adoptive family really began.

My Sources of Strength and Courage

Brian and I resolved to raise our three children with the same values that our parents had nurtured in us. We needed specific goals and planned schedules. I was used to this from all my years as a primary teacher. Now, at last, I could teach and challenge my own children. It was so satisfying.

The children learned to listen respectfully to the Bible, sing songs of praise to God, and make beautiful pictures expressing the sorrow and joy of Jesus' life, death, and resurrection. One Sunday workbook had an activity we used as a permanent family teaching tool. Four pages for coloring and taping together depicted Palm Sunday, the Last Supper, the Agony in the Garden, the Death on the Cross, and the Resurrection. We worked hard at coloring these very carefully. When they were completed on Easter Sunday, I taped them together into a large rectangle and taped the whole thing to their basement playroom wall. Over the rest of their growing years I referred to it often for behavioral goals. I repeated what my mother taught us: "If Jesus could give his life for us, we should be able to give in to each other, too. Then some day we will all enjoy heaven together." Sometimes they appreciated this, and sometimes they resented it. That's life.

Tips For Adoptive Parents

✦ Memorizing good behavior for a future event minimizes embarrassment.

✦ If adopted children ask about their birth parents, answer their questions as simply as possible.

Books, Music, and websites

I used many books and records to teach the children religion, and then gave many of them away so that other children could benefit from them. Some of the recordings were:

⁓ *God's People Give Thanks*, a presentation by Houston's Episcopal Church of the Redeemer Choir recorded by ACA Recording Studios Inc., Houston, Texas.

⁓ The Medical Mission Sisters Series, including: "I Know the Secret," "In Love," "Joy is Like the Rain," "Knock Knock," and "Seasons" from Avant Garde Records Inc., New York, with the music published by The Vanguard Music Corporation. These were our favorites because they were so spirited and yet easy to understand.

⁓ For acceptance of all peoples we included Walt Disney's "It's a Small World." It was sung by the Disneyland Boys Choir. Produced by Camarata, a Walt Disney Production.

⁓ *The Music Machine: an Adventure in Agapeland* is a musical adventure teaching the fruit of the spirit to all ages. It is by Candle, Sparrow Records, Inc.

⁓ Another Agapeland recording we liked (Candle, Sparrow Records, Inc.) was *Bullfrogs & Butterflies*.

Books I used for elementary religious education:

⁓ Weber, Anne. *In the Land of the Music Machine,* and *Return to the Land of the Music Machine.* Elgin, Illinois : Cook Publishing, 1983-84. These books accompanied the Agapeland records. Children like to see pictures while listening and singing.

⁓ McMahon, Bob. *Let Singing Be My Song.* St. Meinrad, Indiana: Abbey Press, 1974. The story of Thrushuska a song bird's struggle to make it. (He does.)

⌐ De Saint Exupery, Antoine. *The Little Prince*. New York: Harcourt, Brace & World, Inc., 1943, 1971. Our children were deeply touched by this tender, heart warming, enchanting fable.

⌐ *The Children's Bible*. New York: Golden Press 1965,1975. Excellent pictures and well written.

⌐ National Geographic Society. *Every Day Life in Bible Times* and *Great Religions of the World*. Beautiful pictures of present day. National Geographic Society: Washington, D.C., 1967, 1973.

⌐ Ideals. *The Story of Easter For Children*. Milwaukee, Wisconsin: Ideals Publishing Corporation, 1984.

⌐ Montgomery, Mary & Herb. *Come to Communion*. Minneapolis, MN: Winston Press, 1973. Each one of our children had their own work books. They have kept them to remember their First Communion Day.

⌐ De Paola, Tomie. *Now One Foot, Now the Other*. New York: G.P. Putnam's Sons, 1981. This book taught our children the value of different stages in our lives. We start out young and we grow old. Each time deserves our respect.

❧ Adopt—features factsheets and links covering open adoption, international adoption, crisis pregnancy, and surrogacy: http://www.adopting.org/

❧ Adoption Classifieds—search the database for children available for adoption or for parents looking to adopt. Place an ad, or find a lawyer to help with an adoption: http://www.adoptionclassifieds.com/

The Happy Years When
Dreams Came True

The next ten years were everything we hoped for in many ways. We had our family routine of Brian going to work, Mary, Tommy and Chris in the various stages of pre-school, kindergarten, elementary school, and middle school. I took them to and from school by car or walking, depending on the weather. We lived one mile from school. We always helped with the homework, and I was active as a member of our school parent-teacher association. At first I published the school paper once a month. Then I became president of the association for several years. I volunteered as a teacher helper for some students needing extra attention. We were always busy. Summers always included morning lessons in phonics, reading, math, and English for all three children. I knew they were going to need an edge to make it—that edge would be a good education.

We also traveled as much as we could by taking four-day mini-vacations once a month when Brian finished his week of third shift. These trips enabled us to see the natural and historic sites of our state and several others close by. I helped them write about these trips. Sometimes we camped out for the weekend and took beautiful nature walks. Fishing was a great source of family fun because we had a trailer at the lake and could stay overnight at a familiar place. We spent many hours of vacation there with Brian's brothers and sisters, nieces and nephews. Each winter we went to this lake for ice-skating, and sometimes brought Mary and Tommy's brother, Steve, and sister, Jenny.

During these years we experienced more good times than bad. When I ask the children about the times they remember, they always surprise me by describing little things going on between them of which Brian and I were not even aware. They seem to have missed historic places altogether, but they remember how scary it was to look down into the Grand Canyon, and exciting to look out the window at Yellowstone National Park at a moose. They have no recollection of riding a canal boat near Piqua, Ohio, but they remember Mount Rushmore quite clearly. Tommy was asked to tickle the tummy of an alligator in the Reptile Gardens near there. We were all afraid the alligator might wake up too soon, but Tommy loved the attention and wasn't afraid. I think this is why they remember this.

A wonderful discovery I made through these years was the value of memories stored in photographs. Each time I got the pictures out from previous years, the feeling of family was more solidified. This was our history—our own story—and the memories were good. The children began to develop a sense of family pride. We had a lot of experiences to share with extended family and friends. We traveled by car, train, and plane to visit family far away and near. The children gradually learned the difference between adoptive relatives and biological ones. In a way, this was disturbing for them. It was confusing. It was especially difficult for Chris, because he didn't know any of his biological relatives, and this caused him to feel "left out." It became an obsession for him to find at least one biological relative.

During these happy years we were unaware of the permanency of the damage that abuse and neglect, and possibly genetics, had done to our three children. But everything that happens to us is stored in our memories forever. We only hoped that their memories would include the many great ones we were adding to their repertoire. However, nothing has more impact on who we are than our genes and our first experiences of life. Although this is a fact we all have to accept, a great deal of hard work and childhood formation can make a big difference, and we worked hard at this.

When Tommy and Chris were ten years old and Mary was fourteen, I needed major surgery that was routine but serious. This meant four days in the hospital and taking things slow and easy for six weeks at home. I was fine, but the children were insecure enough to be traumatized again. Mary and Tom were worried and made unreal demands, but Chris was positive I was going to die. He began to look around school for a new mother. There was a student teacher in his classroom who was married and had no children. She liked Chris and he planned to ask her to adopt him if I died. Of course I didn't die, but this seemed to be the trigger for his ADHD to become more than he could control, and we began to see a psychiatrist. Tommy was also having a hard time concentrating on his schoolwork, and he was diagnosed with the same thing. They both began taking medication. The teen years had begun.

My Sources of Strength and Courage

Abused children take for granted that life is filled with trauma. Not I. Trauma after trauma was wearing me down. Now I understood why these children could turn their emotions on and off like faucets. They had to, for survival. I did not want to become this way, and made a conscious awareness of this possibility and tucked it into my Zen memory bank. During our children's pre-teen and teen years my practice of Zen meditation became more important than ever.

Tips For Adoptive Parents

↵ Getting in touch with their own feelings seems to be one of the biggest challenges for children who have been abused.

Books, Music, and websites

I used the following books, for our children's pre-teen years:

– Wilt, Joy. *Making Up Your Own Mind* and *The Nitty-Gritty of Family Life*, in the *Ready, Set, Grow* series. Waco, Texas: Word, Inc., 1979. These are combination book-work books. They cannot be given away, but are the children's to keep. We used these two. Others in the series are: *You're All Right* (Human similarities), *You're One-of-a-Kind* (Human uniqueness), *Mine and Yours* (Rights and responsibilities), *Saying What You Mean* (Communication skills), *Keeping Your Body Alive and Well* (Physical needs), *Handling Your Ups and Downs* (Emotions), *Needing Each Other* (Relational needs), *A Kid's Guide to Making Friends* (Social skills), *Surviving Fights With Brothers and Sisters* (Sibling rivalry), *A Kid's Guide to Managing Money* (Money management).

– Barclay, William. *Jesus of Nazareth*. Cleveland, Ohio: William Collins & Co.Ltd., 1977. Based on the film directed by Franco Zeffirelli.

⁓ Johnson, M.D., Spencer. *The Value of Kindness: The Story of Elizabeth Fry*. La Jolla, CA: Value Communications, Inc., 1976. I purchased a set of 34 books, each portrays a different value in a real person's life. I read them to our children. Then they re-read them on their own. Cathie liked them so much that she read them many times. They like to read them to this day. The books are simply great! I donated the set to our parish's Religious Ed. Program.

⁓ Caines, Jeannette. *Just Us Women*. New York: Harper & Row, 1982. This book helps children to understand the special relaxed relationship that we can have with a mature loving relative.

❧ School (K - 12) Resources/Info and Parenting Issues—Pat McClendon's Clinical Social Work: URL: http://www.ClinicalSocialWork.com/

Mary Today

15

Although by the time she was eight Mary had overcome the huge emotional hurdle of bonding with us, she still had others to face. She had many physical obstacles to overcome, but these were relatively easy compared to the psychological ones. Mary was fortunate to have an excellent case worker who, for example, responded to my suggestion for a psychiatrist by setting up an appointment immediately when Mary was only four years old. One of the important lessons I learned at this time was about Mary's sensitivity to any display of anger on my part. Her psychiatrist told me that Mary lost control easily if she thought I was angry, and I learned the importance of keeping as cool and calm as possible.

When Mary first came to us she could not hear, see, or speak very well. Throughout her growing up years she had many different counselors and doctors. She had myopia in her right eye, so her left eye was doing all the work. Her eye doctor prescribed glasses and a patch over the left eye. This helped a little, but not much. Next we tried eye therapy, which helped more, but still did not prevent the crossing of her right eye. The problem was finally solved when she began wearing contacts in the fifth grade.

Contacts were a big thing for her. She was noticeably prettier, and she could see much better, but eventually the mechanics of getting them in and out, cleaned and stored, were more than she could handle. She wanted to do it all herself, and we hoped she could. But, in fact, she lost or chipped over five hundred dollars worth of lenses, and we realized that was more than we could afford. I put the lenses in for her each day for about a year, until she decided that good looks were just not worth the pain. Now she wears her regular glasses.

Her hearing and speech problems went together, of course. We took her to an ear, nose and throat specialist who was gentle and patient, and Mary did everything he said. He prescribed ear drops for six weeks, a non-dairy diet, and therapy at school. The speech therapist at school helped Mary talk quietly and clearly instead of shouting. Apparently Mary had caused white nodules to grow on her vocal cords by shouting and screaming, which, in turn, produced her husky voice. Her therapist did a great job. It all worked: the earwax loosened and was removed by the doctor, the white nodules on her vocal cords disappeared by her tenth year, and Mary could hear and speak correctly. Both her doctor and therapist were thrilled with her success, and Brian and I were credited with patient perseverance on her behalf.

When she was eight she was having a lot of trouble getting along with her two brothers. Instead of playing cooperatively with them, she insisted on having her way—and so, of course, did they. They fought and cried so much that I had to separate them most of the time. I asked Mary's social worker about this, and Jean set up a test with a very good psychologist in the area. The psychologist noticed that Mary responded well to my visible presence at all times. She needed to know that I was not going to leave her. Each time Mary felt stressed, she would shake her head with a tick-like movement. The tick would continue until she heard me say, "You are okay, Mary. I'm here and you are doing fine." The psychologist thought that Mary would have a chance if she were to stay with us, and this was all the confirmation we needed. Our plans for adoption went forward.

In addition, the tests showed that Mary could learn well if she was shown a pattern. I knew that music was essentially a series of patterns, so I immediately started her on piano lessons. She loved it and did well. One day she played a song she had watched me play for about a month. She used both hands and played it without missing a note. I was flabbergasted. I now realized just how gifted she was at copying patterns.

Two years later Mary decided to play violin in the elementary school orchestra. She had to work hard at it, but ended up playing with the other students. I asked her to play some Christmas songs for my Writer's Club Christmas Party. She did this along with her brother, Tommy. One of the club members was a violinist in our city orchestra, who volunteered to become their violin teacher. Her weekly visits gave Mary much needed encouragement and advice. This violin teacher has been responsible for much of Mary's success; she continues to give Mary lessons, and is one of her best friends.

Mary progressed in spurts, and still does. In high school, Mary received many awards for her achievements in orchestra. We attended all of her concerts, and taped some of them. Now she loves country music so much that she hopes to be able to join a country band some day. Since that would mean many hours of playing the violin each day, she decided to practice for several hours after work. After some weeks, her teacher noticed the improvement and complimented her. Mary's confidence grew and she volunteered to play for church services. Much to everyone's surprise she did it beautifully, and continues to contribute her talents at church once a month. This is a source of great pride for her, the violin teacher, and us.

Another boost from her therapist involved the practice of counting to ten when frustrated. Mary did this faithfully. Then one day, after counting to ten, she came to me and said, "I'm just going to leave when Chris and Tommy are mean to me." When I told her therapist, she was thrilled to know that Mary could start solving her own problems.

As a school student Mary was a joy to her teachers. She was able to maintain a "C" average with the help of special education resources. By the fifth grade she was doing so well that she graduated from special education temporarily.

The middle school years were challenging and difficult, but Mary worked unbelievably hard to please her teachers, and I helped her every step of the way. Her teachers loved and admired her. They always gave Brian and me a lot of credit for helping her. It helped to make these years happy and worth while. Mary really enjoyed school.

Mary became proficient on the computer, which she used for games and homework assignments. Sometimes her work looked so professional we had to include her original hand written copy so that her teachers could see Mary had done the work. She loved surprising her teachers in this manner. Math was always her hardest subject. We assured her that many people have this same problem. When she got frustrated with her homework, and started to yell and cry and say she wanted to quit, Brian and I calmly helped her, and on she went.

Mary began her teen behavior around her freshman year in high school. She struggled hard to do her work, but felt lost. We helped her and she co-operated with us, but her biggest problem was in getting along with other students. They openly ridiculed her for being retarded. She learned to stand her ground by telling them that harassment was against the law and she would report them if they did it again. They left her alone—too alone. But although Mary had no friends at school, during the summer she went swimming and met some friends at the pool. They invited her to come to their church social events for teens, and this was a lifesaver.

As a high school freshman, Mary tried to do too much. She wanted to learn Spanish, in addition to the required subjects, to fulfill the college entrance requirement. One night she started crying and screaming that she did not want to live. I told her that she needed to talk to a school counselor. I went with her and explained her situation. He was very good at his job, and set up a staffing with all of her teachers and some county social workers. He did this in just a few hours.

Mary was tested and placed once more in the special education program. This provided the necessary support, and she was relieved. We also assured her that she did not have to take Spanish now in order to keep alive her dream of college, so she gratefully dropped it and from then on had a much more manageable schedule. Not many other students were understanding and friendly, and she was quite lonely during this time.

One of Mary's dreams was to be a nurse's aide. Since our school system is affiliated with a Career Development Center, we encouraged Mary to take a nursing class to see if she liked it. After about six weeks her instructor suggested that she look at a different profession. It seemed to her that Mary would not be able to work independently, as nursing required.

This opened up the world of restaurant careers for her. She loved this class, and her teacher treasured her hard work and serious effort. When her senior year was coming to an end, her teacher asked if she would think about getting hired as a teacher's aide for this class. She did. However, by the time school started in the fall, the teacher had moved and was replaced by a very demanding male chef. He made the year difficult for Mary but she honored her contract and completed the year.

True to her dream, Mary did enroll in community college. She completed one class during the summer following graduation. Then she enrolled during the school year. Both Math and English proved too challenging for her. We praised her for going as long as she did. She still might try again later.

From the time Mary was sixteen, she worked. Her first job was at McDonald's. Her manager was wonderful and encouraged her to try everything. We were amazed. She was able to do everything except become a manager, which she did not want to try because she knew it would be too upsetting. She worked for them off and on for five years.

Wanting to try other jobs, she spent short periods of time as a courtesy clerk in a grocery store and as an assembly line packager. She had many difficulties because of her slowness and allergies, as well as complaining customers. So when she heard that the male chef was no longer teaching, and the new teacher wanted her help, she went back to her old job. She is still there as a teacher's aide, and loves it. She plans to stay for at least ten years. But Mary knew that she would also need a summer job because this one paid only when the students were present, so she worked at McDonald's during the summer. The pressures eventually got to her, and she decided to find a different job.

She began looking for other options in the classifieds, and noticed a lot of ads for nurses' aides. The county agency encouraged her to take a class. She passed the class at the nursing home, but then had to pass state tests in order to be certified. When she did not pass the state tests she decided to stop working at the nursing home. We praised her for trying.

Around this time Mary's therapist came to our home for family therapy. The value of this therapy can never be measured—Mary progressed so well. Unfortunately, funding was cut off and the therapy ended. Mary now receives help from safety counselors and her cooking helper and job coach from the Developmental Disabilities Center. She feels very loved with this attention from kind and caring people.

When Mary graduated from high school, she wanted to get her own apartment because she heard other graduates talking about it. So we went apartment or home hunting to see how ready she really was. We found a good brick home close to one of Brian's sisters, but as we walked around in the empty house with a real estate lady, she said, "I don't want a house. It scares me."

So we looked for apartments that would be affordable and safe. Finally we found one that she thought would be just right. She filled out an application for it, turned it in, and waited— only to be turned down. The apartment owner told her that she thought it would be too hard for her to pay the rent. Mary was disappointed and decided to drop the idea for the time being, but Brian and I were relieved because we did not feel she was ready for this kind of independence. Her high school counselor agreed with us.

Two years later we met a sweet young woman who was going to need a roommate soon. This was the opportunity Mary needed. They were both happy with the arrangement. After much checking with county agencies, Mary was given the go ahead and moved out of our home into her first new home. She was excited and we were happy for her. The distance from us was the only damper on her happiness—she was about five miles from home. We kept in close touch by phone and visits.

Gradually, the two roommates got on each other's nerves, and Mary wanted her very own apartment closer to our home. We were not too happy with this idea because we thought she was safer living with a roommate, but she insisted that she didn't need one. So, once more we went apartment hunting. Since Mary qualified for government help, we had to find apartments that accepted their subsidy and all of the accompanying paperwork.

Fortunately, Mary found a very nice one that filled the bill for all of her needs, and after living one and a half years with a roommate she moved into her own apartment. She lived alone there for nine months before admitting that it was just too lonely. At that point her brother, Tommy, decided he was now ready to move out, too, so he moved into the other bedroom. They had problems getting along from time to time; Tommy didn't like living with his sister, and decided to find his own apartment. This was fine with Mary—she got an apartment across from his, and now they are quite content. Mary likes the security of having a brother close, and Tom likes Mary's company each day after work. We visit them often because they love the attention and security.

For five years Mary drove her own vehicle. It boosted her ego during high school, and gave her a lot of self-confidence. However, if she drove while she was upset, she was easily distracted. After several minor accidents she had her insurance dropped and her license revoked. We were all relieved. Now she travels all over by bus or us, and she likes feeling safe.

Successful independence for Mary at last.

Mary loves sports and music. She plays on the Special Olympics teams for softball and bowling. She cheers for her choice of professional teams and goes to any games she can. Many county agencies offer chances for recreation. She takes advantage of these where she feels comfortable. She can do these activities independently, and this is good for her.

Mary is now concentrating on having more of a social life by signing up with a group called "Out and About." Participants are taken places every Friday evening for social events such as dinner, theater, park recreation or laser games. Some events are fun for her and others are not. Her usual pattern for participation in such programs has been an enthusiastic start, mellowing down after a few problems arise, and then quitting for a while. We just share in her emotion at the time, whatever it happens to be.

My Sources of Strength and Encouragement

I read many books to help Mary with her problems. Each time her doctor put her on a diet, I went to the library or bookstore for more information so that I could understand as much as possible about what was happening to her. It helped me to actively seek information about Mary's condition.

Tips For Adoptive Parents

↞ Abused children need a lot of help recognizing the difference between fantasy and reality. This is huge. Start early explaining the difference.

Books, Music, and Websites

— Smith, Lendon H., M.D. *Improving Your Child's Behavior Chemistry*. New York: Pocket Books, 1977 (a Simon & Schuster division of Gulf and Western Corporation, 1230 Avenue of the Americas, New York, N.Y. 10020). This book contained specific ideas for raising children with emotional problems by giving them a helpful diet. It made the difference we needed at the time. I think that each age has its own self-help ideas. Another good book for me was:

— L. Ron Hubbard. *Child Dianetics*. Los Angeles: Church of Scientology of California, 1976. (2723 West Temple ST, Los Angeles, CA 90026). I liked the soothing self-control this book fostered, but I disagree with its policy toward medication and psychiatry. Obviously, our children have benefitted greatly from both.

❧ Adoption Counselor.com—adoption counselors can add their listing, and the public can search for a counselor and submit queries. Also features chat and message boards: http://www.adoptioncounselor.com/

❧ Adoption Search—find a search engine dedicated to adoptee searches, and to general resources on related topics, such as pregnancy and infertility: http://www.adoptionsearch.com/

— Lifton, Betty Jean. *Lost and Found, Twice Born, And I'm Still Me.* New York: Dial Press, 1979. This is about the right of all of us to know our own identity.

Tommy Today

Tommy was pleasant and cooperative throughout most of his childhood. He was very nonchalant and quiet, but his quietness may have been accepted too easily by all of us. We can now see that it gets in the way of his socializing. He is so shy with everyone except his family that he can't get jobs or go out with young ladies without help.

He may have sustained brain damage from his skull fracture at nine months—no one knows. His learning disability caused him to struggle with schoolwork, but we helped him each night. English was his strongest subject, and he was happy with his ability to express his opinions in writing. As long as he was helped with an interview style, he wrote good poems and book reviews for English. All through elementary school he received speech therapy, and he gradually learned to speak clearly. He needed to slow down his speech instead of slurring all his words together.

In the primary grades Tommy had been easily distracted by other students, so Brian made him a special three-sided secretary box for privacy while working on his papers. This worked for the primary years. By the time he reached fourth and fifth grades we were having monthly visits with a psychiatrist to help with his behavior, which was sometimes out of control. We used ritalin for two years, but it did not seem to be what Tom needed. We started him on lithium, and that helped him control his behavior.

Tom always loved sports and music. He went into the fourth-grade phase of collecting with great enthusiasm. He began with football cards and expanded into every team sport. He collected and traded cards, miniature helmets, posters, and magazines. After reading the stories of great athletes, he talked to us and school friends endlessly about them. He memorized the statistics, and we were amazed at his ability to remember and spit them out at a moment's notice. They were usually accurate. When he was wrong, he said, "Who cares?"

Having just the right sports clothes became a big thing for him, and we finally had to get across to him that all things have to be limited. Only millionaires get to buy every item in every collection they start.

Playing softball, bowling, basketball, and running track became opportunities to be just like his favorite idols in each sport. After watching his idols play he imitated their techniques and did so well that he surprised everyone, including himself. Participating in these sports was so important to him that he refused to get a job that would interfere with them. Once I realized this, I made sure with his employer that he could have the right days off for his sports. Brian and I knew that there was no other way he would keep a job.

Tommy's musical talents were developed with three different instruments, the first being the piano. As he improved over the years, he filled our home with beautiful music. One night Brian said, "Is that Tommy playing?" It was so smooth and soothing. We complimented him and thanked him, and I sometimes recorded him when he didn't know. (Tommy does not perform well when he knows we are observing; he wants us to share in his successes secretly and we try to comply.) Each year he was expected to play at a recital. Eventually, he felt too old for this and stopped playing the piano.

He began violin the summer after fourth grade—the traditional time to join the school orchestra or band. He played in the orchestra until his sophomore year in high school. We were so delighted to see him play at his sister's commencement exercises, which happened at the end of his freshman year. He received a wonderful achievement award for that year in the orchestra, and continued with his lessons each week along with Mary. Then he asked his violin teacher if she would teach him how to play the classical guitar.

She helped him learn the basics on a guitar we gave him for Christmas. After that she found a great teacher for him, and he played for two years. He learned to imitate his country music idols just as he imitated his sports idols, and his teacher helped him record some of his music on a cassette tape. We played his music as we opened our Christmas gifts the next year, and it was wonderfully peaceful.

It was around this time that Tom began accompanying Mary to church social events with the friends she had met at the swimming pool. Even though Tom was much younger, he went along with his sister because Mary's friends liked him. For about six years they went swimming, skiing, and pool playing at their church events. I was disappointed that our own church did not accept teens with disabilities as generously as did that of their friends. The adults in our church accepted them with admiration, but the teens did not follow the example of their parents and leaders. Tom kept the friends from our neighboring church until his senior year in high school, when their schedules conflicted and Tom ceased to make any effort to see them. At this time he spent every free minute with his older biological sibling, Steve, who lived in his own home. We tried and tried at family therapy to help Tom understand that too much time together was not good for either one of them. He refused to listen and had several temper tantrums before deciding not to see Steve so much.

During one of these tantrums, Tom broke his beautiful classical guitar to smithereens. He said it felt good. He was disappointed with his inability to play it as well as his idols, Vince Gill and Randy Travis.

He spent many hours listening to country music and watching recordings of all the country western awards shows. Tom sometimes went with Mary to the country western line dances in town. Mary danced with abandon, but Tom just watched. He read everything he could get his hands on that had to do with the famous western singers and actors. He would love to be a singer, too, but he would not be able to endure taking voice lessons. He said he would be way too embarrassed.

Socially, Tommy had the help of group therapy in elementary school. He learned how to make friends. In middle school he put these skills to good use by sticking close to three good friends. They ate together in the cafeteria and helped each other with homework, but after high school they saw very little of each other. Everyone encouraged Tom to socialize more, but no one could compare with his brother, Steve, when it came to having a friend. They shared their love of collections, music, and sports. They still play on the same teams, and attend the same events. Steve has his own residence now, 30 miles away, and loves to have Tom over.

Learning to drive was rather easy for Tom. He took the driving course in high school and got a job after school so he could buy his own truck, which he drove to work and to his brother's home each day. This truck came home with dents and flat tires for a couple of years, and then he totaled it. No one was injured and he was able to buy a used car. This independence has been very important to him.

When Tom was in middle school he attended an assembly that featured a computer expert. The speaker encouraged students to take computer classes in order to ensure job security later. Tom went for every computer class he could take for the next six years. At the end of his senior year, he heard of a computer job that was available, filled out the application, and had an interview for the job, along with many other applicants. Tom did not get the job. He was stunned, and never applied for another computer job. He would like to take more computer classes some day.

In Tom's mind, two important job criteria have always been that he be able to play his sports, and that he be safe. His first job was with our school system as a sweep boy. He did well as long as he stayed in near proximity to the janitor. But if he got left to clean a huge building alone and late at night, he was too scared to do the job and he quit. Years later he realized that if he stayed with a difficult job, he could have better offers later. He went through job after job, and kept quitting instead of telling anyone that he was scared. No one knew what his needs were because he didn't communicate them. Finally, Brian and I found out by gradually putting together his comments.

He didn't know, himself, why he was quitting until we went over and over his comments about each job. After a year of this we decided that we would have to advocate for him. He was too discouraged with his inability to make it at work. When he got frustrated with a job he tried as a nurse's aide, he drove off to a mall parking lot and went to sleep in his truck. His work supervisor called to ask where he was. It was about 7:00 a.m. on a cold winter day, and Brian and I got up, dressed and went looking for him. We saw his truck sitting in the parking lot at our mall about three miles from home, and he was in it, sound asleep. When we woke him, he said he couldn't do the job any more. To make matters worse, he had run his truck battery down and needed to have it re-charged. We took Tom to his workplace and helped him apologize and resign correctly.

Another time, when he was exhausted from trying to work in a fast foods restaurant, he went to his brother's home for a rest. He was so uptight that he lost control and began throwing his things out of his brother's house. He had gradually taken many of his belongings to his brother's house because he wanted to move in with him after graduation.

Steve was alarmed by his lack of control and called us. We told him to call the police and we would be there. We went and found him sitting on his brother's lawn with papers, tapes, and equipment strewn all around him. Two officers were talking to him. He was shaking with fear. I asked Tom what the problem was and he said he couldn't take being put down any more. He did not want to live. I explained to the officers the best I could about Tom's mental condition. They said that they would have to cuff him and take him to the hospital for an evaluation. We agreed and followed him there. After several hours of waiting, and finally seeing a psychiatrist and agreeing to set up some therapy sessions for Tom, we took him home. Tom's hopes for independence with his brother were dashed. Now he was so upset he didn't want to see his brother anymore.

I went with him to his therapy sessions. His therapist came up with a great idea for him. She helped him see that his life was more positive than he thought by having him evaluate each day on a scale from one to ten. This was right up his alley with his love for statistics, and he improved quickly. He finished high school one month later, and graduated on a positive note. We had a nice celebration, which everyone enjoyed. He behaved well, and no one knew what he was suffering except us. He felt so much better from the positive attention that he seemed to forget his troubles with Steve.

Tom has told us that sometimes he doesn't care about anyone or anything. But, he said when he thinks about things later, he is very grateful that we adopted him and that he is a part of our family. He admits to being too afraid of dying to ever kill himself. He just wants some employer to understand him and hire him. It's a tall order to understand him, but who knows? Maybe someday it will happen. My faith says it will.

Many employers won't talk to a parent of a special needs adult, but we eventually found one who was understanding and did talk to me. As a result, Tom got a good farming job at a goat dairy business. He liked working out in the country with patient people and the baby goats, and especially enjoyed the days when he got to feed the babies. It was a fun job, but it was only for a few hours a week. The small paychecks discouraged him, and he quit.

Tom's pattern of quitting jobs abruptly, apparently the result of his shy inability to communicate with anyone clearly, continued for seven more jobs. Most of the time it takes several weeks for him to know, himself, why he has quit. Now that he has the help of a government organization called "Job Link," we hope he can put an end to this pattern of behavior. Our biggest concern is that he be able to keep a job, because if Tom doesn't stay busy during the day he gets very bored. A county agency is supplying him with a job coach to help him keep his job, and also help with communication problems. He now has a part time job at a pizza restaurant where he feels understood and likes the work. We are happy for him.

Today Tom is a contented and grateful young man.

Tom is now in his own apartment, which is just across the sidewalk from Mary's apartment in the same complex where they had lived together previously. He thinks he has learned enough from Mary in six months to enable him to be complete-ly independent, and we hope he is right. So far, he is doing well, and this does seem to be a good arrangement. Tom likes for us to call him to see how he is doing. He also likes for us to visit him and make sure everything is going well. Mary can't boss him around in his own apartment, and yet he likes for her to come over for visits each day.

My Sources of Strength and Courage

As time passed and we realized that Tom, Mary, and Chris were all going to have permanent disabilities, we felt stunned. Then we looked at life from the perspective of ability rather than disability. Considering the worldviews of different people and their many different abilities, we believed that our children were considerably blessed. We thanked God that they all had healthy bodies. I mentioned it often and thanked God for it with joy. Soon Tom followed our example, verbally thanking Brian and me for all that we have done, and continue to do, for him, Mary, and Chris. This is so gratifying. It makes the strug-gles all worth while.

Since Tom admires so many Country Western singers, he wants to copy them spiritually. This is another blessing. He likes Gospel songs. He reads his own Bible to learn more about what inspires these singers and songwriters.

My simple pattern of early meditation and asking my par-ents and grandparents in heaven to inspire all of us to be good people remains the same. I keep pictures of my family and my little country church on my piano in our living room. Each morning I center myself and go about my chores and senior vol-unteer jobs in peace and joy. Life is good.

I would also like to mention the help that Brian and I found from another quarter. We had felt so helpless and alone in our efforts to help Tom. Our church spontaneously developed a support group for caretakers of people with mental illness, and I decided to attend one of these meetings to test its appropriateness for us. It was wonderful! I was introduced to the organization known as NAMI, the National Alliance for the Mentally Ill. This organization consists of thousands of families who are going through the same experiences we are. The organization teaches classes about mental illnesses and how to cope. Brian and I attended these classes for twelve Saturdays. It was such a relief to know we were not alone. We have had more understanding and patience with Tom since we joined this helpful organization. We highly recommend it for anyone who feels helpless or hopeless about a family member who may be mentally ill or, more correctly stated, may have a chemical imbalance. Anyone interested in this organization can get help by calling 1-703-524-7600–FAX 703-524-9094 or by e-mailing http://www.nami.org or writing to National Alliance for the Mentally Ill at 200 N. Glebe Road, Suite 1015, Arlington, VA 22203-3754.

Tips For Adoptive Parents

✦ When deciding whether or not to adopt, try to imagine yourself in the child's shoes. If you still care, you should probably adopt.

Books, Music, and Websites

– Close, Rev. James J. *No One to Call Me Home*. Chicago, Illinois: Mission Press, 1990. Each night during the teen years I read one of these stories and discussed it with our children. I wanted them to appreciate their secure and warm home.

- Adoption Yellow Pages—directory of online adoption resources, including attorneys, agencies, international resources and facilitators: http://www.adoptionyellowpages.com/

Chris Today

12

Chris was precocious, and by the age of three was made aware by rude stares that he was different from the rest of our family: he was Hispanic. We loved him and hoped that would be enough. He asked me if he came from my tummy, and I told him that he came from a different mommy's tummy. He was upset by this and could not be comforted with any stories from adoption books for children.

As he grew up, he always wondered what his birth family was like. We answered his questions and tried to convince him that he was fortunate to be adopted. His birth mother, who was German and Cherokee, looked like a typical Anglo-Saxon. His birth father was Hispanic, and Chris looks like him. He was surprised, years later, when he saw that his birth mother looked more like us than him, and we were never able to convince him that looks did not matter.

School was both challenging and fun. He was bright and could do his papers easily, but he was distracted and often forgot to finish his work. His teachers enjoyed his cheerful disposition, but wondered about his hyper-sensitivity and impulsive reaction to other students. He was always looking for a close friend to stick by him, and by the fourth grade he found one.

It was during this time that I had surgery, and Chris became extremely insecure and began acting out at school. We went together, as a family, to a psychiatrist. We charted behavior and set up a system of rewards, and he began taking Ritilan. Chris was making progress until the psychiatrist moved and was replaced by another—a good and understanding doctor, but Chris seemed to feel abandoned by the first doctor and would not cooperate with the new one.

By the time Chris was ten he wanted to play all the video games that were available. I didn't think they were good for him, so we played only the computer games that were more academic than violent. He began asking other students at school which games they played and could he join them? They didn't mind, and invited him over without our knowledge. One day he came home from school and went out to play with the neighbors for a while, and then went several blocks away to play video games with strangers.

None of our family knew where he was. We looked everywhere we could think of, and then, once it got dark, called the police. They helped us search for about a half-hour and then Chris just came walking home as if nothing had happened. One of the officers asked him why he didn't come home or let us know where he was. He said he just wanted to play video games and lost track of time.

Brian and I thought it better for him to have a video game of his own than to do this, so we got one. He played it for a couple of months and then got tired of it. He wanted to stay over with other boys, so we met the parents of his acquaintances and set up his first stay-over. Although it was scary for him he wanted to keep doing it, but he didn't seem to get along with the boys and wasn't invited back.

He was not doing his schoolwork well and he began to smoke cigarettes. We grounded him for this, but he seemed to like provoking us. We couldn't understand what he was trying to tell us. His psychiatrist thought it was just looking for independence in spurts.

When it was time for middle school Chris was afraid to go to the large public school, so we enrolled him in a small private one along with Tommy, who was in the same grade. They started out well, but after the third quarter we realized that Tommy could not get the help he needed, and we transferred him back to the big public school. Chris continued in this school for another year, but by the last quarter of seventh grade he had stopped doing any schoolwork.

When we had a staffing and he was told that he would have to leave the school, he could not believe us. He threatened to stand in front of a truck and get killed. This was the beginning of a series of short mental hospital stays. His psychiatrist changed his medication to lithium and he calmed down. However, this was also the beginning of a big weight gain—he no longer felt handsome. Lithium also caused him to shake when he tried to do difficult tasks, and this embarrassed and frustrated him.

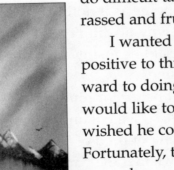

One of Chris's many mountain paintings

I wanted Chris to have something positive to think about and look forward to doing. I asked him what he would like to do, and he told me he wished he could paint pictures. Fortunately, there were teachers in the area who gave painting lessons once a month. They worked with a local hobby shop, so Chris signed up for lessons and began creating beautiful oil paintings each month. He was hard on himself and found fault with each painting, but I praised him and bought them in order to frame and treasure them.

The classes lasted five hours, and Chris had been bringing a friend to talk to while he painted. At one point his teachers told him that he could not bring his friend to class, and he reluctantly quit. He began acting out with threatening body language, and at times he was mean to his best friend. We didn't know that his friend's mother had an alcohol problem. Chris began drinking, along with smoking, as a part of his teenage rebellion. Then his best friend's mother refused to let her son spend time with him.

I home schooled him for his eighth grade. He did well when he put his mind to doing his work, but much of his energy went into figuring out how to have fun. Unfortunately, sports were not fun for him. Neither was music, although he tried to play the trumpet and later an electric guitar. He began hanging out with kids who had dropped out of school.

Chris often felt as if kids treated him unfairly because of his Hispanic background. One day when this happened, Chris made the mistake of trying to force a boy to treat him fairly. He pulled out a pocketknife and threatened him. When the threatened boy's mother informed me I begged her to call the police. She refused. I knew I would have to do it myself if we were to help Chris control his impulsive behavior, so I did. This was the beginning of a series of legal problems for Chris.

He was given every possible benefit of the doubt in many probation infractions, but nothing seemed to help him want to do school work with a serious mind. All he could think of was finding his birth family and living with them, but no one knew where they were. Chris was placed in an alternative high school for high-risk youth, and at times he did well. We attended weekly therapy sessions at this school. Goals were set and met until a new program for high-risk youth added more classes to Chris's already full schedule, and the demand was more than he could do. He gave up in frustration, not caring about himself.

Of all the children, Chris had the most difficulty with his teen years. They were so tumultuous for all of us that I could probably write an entire book about them. In order to avoid too much negative attention, I always minimized his bad behavior, but he was in and out of the hospital and juvenile detention so many times that I eventually lost count. As he seemed incapable of learning from his mistakes, Brian and I wracked our brains for solutions. The county agencies co-operated with us, and our insurance company helped tremendously by providing care for his emotional needs. He took his medication for a while and then decided to quit. His friends didn't think he needed any-thing, and the medication was causing him to gain so much weight that he was being ridiculed. In our opinion, Chris never had real friends. We consider a friend to be someone who brings out the best in us, but it seemed that all of Chris's so-called friends used and discarded him, as he did them.

At age 16 he told us he was going to drive whether we taught him or not, so I thought the lesser of two evils would be to teach him how to drive safely. I purchased the same books that Mary and Tommy had used at their school, and went through all of the lessons and hours of practice driving. He took his test at the driving bureau and passed. He got his license.

Although he drove carefully at first, he gradually got more and more careless. Just six months after he got his license, Chris was out drinking and driving. He rolled Brian's truck and went through the windshield, landing on his shoulder. He got right up out of the ditch to save his passenger who was pinned in the truck. We received the call every parent dreads from one of his acquaintances. I really thought it was a prank. I could not believe it was real, but when I went to the hospital to wait for the ambulance, I knew it was. I recognized his feet on the stretcher as they were bringing him out of the ambulance. I wanted to see if he was conscious, so I called out to him, "Chris, I am here. You're going to be alright." He yelled very loudly, "Mom, I love you." I knew he had to be in fairly good condition to be able to say this. I went around to the entrance and phoned Brian. He joined me for hours of trauma. Chris had broken his scapula and was in terrible pain. As he was turned for the x-rays he had blood streaming every which way over his face and arms. He screamed pathetically. Once he got back to a room for cleaning the gravel out of his wounds, I could smell the alcohol. Brian and I were angry. He was breaking every law he could and more of our own family rules. We felt that he was fortunate to be alive; we felt blessed and hoped that Chris had learned from this experience. We were relieved that his license had been taken away and he could no longer drive.

The accident was about the fifth violation of his probation, so he received additional community service. When he failed to complete his service on time he went to juvenile detention for over a month. He thought it was the end of the world, and promised his "stupid" days were over. But they were not. He continued to make one mistake after the other, and ended up doing a two-month stint in a state boot camp. This he liked. If his probation officer had been well she might have lined up a Job Corps school for him, but due to an illness she was gone before she could prepare an after boot camp program.

When Chris returned he stayed close to us and talked about how much he had changed. This lasted for six days, and then he went right back to his old friends and habits. He was now seventeen, and refused to spend much time at home. He hated our rules for regular eating and sleeping. We kept trying to line up jobs for him, but he would work a few days and quit. We also wanted him to graduate, but he stopped doing any schoolwork. A judge placed him in a group home. He ran away. Then he said he was having a nervous break down and was placed in the mental hospital again.

When he went back to the judge, she told him in exasperation that his probation was finished. He was shocked—he couldn't get to her any more. Now he wanted to live in a group home of his own choosing. We knew a woman who had invited him to come into her group home, so we agreed and paid his room and board. After a couple of months he was eighteen and able to get his driver's license back.

We agreed that if he attended school we would continue room and board. He enrolled in some skills classes at the Career Development Center, but never attended. Instead, he lost his temper and hit a girl at the group home, and the woman reluctantly told him he had to leave. He refused to come home and live according to a regular schedule, but moved in with another family who accepted people off the street. We could not understand him. I felt as if I didn't know him at all. I was trying desperately to find his birth family in order to fill what seemed to be a hole in his heart. I was sure that the loveable little boy we knew was inside him somewhere.

I had been searching for three and a half years for one of his birth relatives, when at last I found a connection through his mother's and his aunt's marriage records. One of the marriage witnesses was still in the area and knew where they lived, but they were out of state. Chris couldn't wait to see someone who was actually related to him. I helped him pack his things, and when we drove away a new friend of his came along to help him start a new life in a new state with a new family. I wanted to cry, but I knew I needed to help him face the reality of his past.

Tommy came along so that Brian could stay home in case Mary needed any help. It rained most of the way there, and as we approached the town I asked Chris to call his grandmother. She had a phone and we had our cell phone with us. She was happy to hear from him, but didn't want Chris to stay—just visit. But he was determined to stay. He said that was what he had wanted all his life, and now he was going to do it.

I started for his birth mother's address, and Chris began to sweat and feel faint. I said, "we are going to get this done now," and kept going. We found her apartment and saw Chris's young brother in the front yard. I asked him what his name was and introduced myself and Chris. Chris shook his hand. We looked up and saw his mother and aunt come out the front door. Chris and his mother just looked at each other in silence, and I said, "For heavens sakes, hug each other." They did. His mother invited us in and kept apologizing to Chris for not keeping him as a baby.

Chris's mother said she did not have room for both Chris and his friend, so I went to find an apartment for the boys. They promised to get jobs and be self-supporting by the next month's rent. We all spent the night at a motel because the apartment had no utilities hooked up yet. After getting the necessary beds, dishes and hookups the next day, Tommy and I left in tears.

Chris cried and told me that I would always be his mother, because I had raised and loved him.

We talked on the phone each day. He didn't get a job, and in about six weeks he was in jail. He said he would never do a favor for anybody again. One of his birth mother's friends asked him to drive her car into a wall for her, and he did. Now he was really sorry. He wanted to change his life for good, and we kept hoping that he would. He began to take correspondence courses to finish high school, and we hope that maybe he will graduate some day. With his natural talent for art and his quick mind for video games, he thinks maybe he could become a commercial artist with the use of a computer. He is also interested in becoming an auto mechanic, body repairman, cabinetmaker, or a construction worker. With the right training, he could become any of these.

Since Chris moved away we have been very encouraged to receive birthday and thank you cards from him. It has always been extremely difficult for him to motivate and organize himself enough to do such things. We know each of these cards takes a great effort, and is therefore a sign of great love.

Chris now accepts the reality of his mental illness, which seems to be a family trait. He is the fifth generation in a family that is dependent on alcohol. He wants to stop the cycle. He can see that his alcoholic family is unpredictable, and that he cannot count on them when he needs help. At the same time, he knows that we are always there for him, and has decided that he wants to be like us.

We have advised him many times to go to Job Corps, and he finally agreed that this would be his best option for getting a diploma and a job skill. He asked us to help him move close to a Job Corps site, and before moving he called his birth mother and brother to ask them to take care of his cats. They agreed to do this, and when they came to pick up the cats and say goodbye, Chris's mother told him to thank Brian and me for raising him, and for continuing to take such good care of him. She wished she could have done this for him, but knew she couldn't.

What a blessing this was! Now, Chris had his birth mother's permission to love us and allow us to be his parents again. It was very much like when Mary decided to love us and join our family. We noticed an emotional maturity in Chris that had been missing before. This was what he needed—now he is ready to move on with his life, and we have more hope for his ability to become an independent, responsible, and happy person.

Now Chris knows he can love us.

My Sources of Strength and Courage

Chris, Tom, and Mary are all grateful that we adopted them. Mary often says that she wishes she had been born to us, but since she wasn't, at least she had the next best thing by being raised by us. They are loving and sweet to us when life is not too frustrating for them. When it is, they use bad language and say nasty things to us, which we ignore. We have learned never to take anything personally when they are upset. An hour later they act as if nothing happened. Brian and I are very happy to have given our children as much independence as possible. They are all doing well under the circumstances of their disabilities, which are not as prominent as their abilities. We always expect a lot from them, and they usually do well and we feel blessed.

The teen years were more difficult than we could ever have dreamed. We thought Chris would graduate from high school and go to college to become an engineer or commercial artist. Just as many parents have dashed dreams for their children, so did we. Chris had a whole world of his own going on in his head, which we could not comprehend. I tried many times to get into his world, but could not. He broke the law for fun. Living a disciplined life seemed so boring to him that he preferred taking his chances with exciting choices, even though he knew it was hard for us when we had to go with him to juvenile court.

At that time I repeatedly asked our church friends to pray for him, to inspire him to make better choices. Each morning at meditation, I ended with a heartfelt prayer to my relatives in heaven asking for inspiring ideas for Chris. He never did anything that completely ruined his life, and, looking at the range of possibilities, we are very grateful for that. Now he is learning to be more responsible for himself. He made it through the most difficult teen years and now is in his twenties. One day at a time—he says he surprises himself with progress.

Tips For Adoptive Parents

↩ The correct school can be the key to success for a disturbed child. If it seems too expensive, compare other costs if needs are not met, and then decide.

↩ Even though a child has been abused, s/he needs to have her/his parents' permission to love other parents. If this does not happen, openly discuss feelings about it.

Books, Music, and Websites

— Previte, Mary Taylor. *Hungry Ghosts*. Grand Rapids, Michigan: Zondervan Publishing House, a division of Harper Collins Publishing, 1994. This book was helpful in understanding some of Chris's thinking. I was amazed at how much of his teen age thinking was influenced by his genetic background. However, I clung firmly to the reality of our years of love and goodness winning in his maturing mind. I was right.

— Michener, James A. *Iberia* and *Mexico*. New York: Random House, 1968 and 1992. These two books gave me insight into some of Chris's genetic background. I was able to discuss these with Chris.

❧ Adoption.com—find guides for birth mothers considering giving up their child for adoption, for adoptees looking for family, and for parents wanting to adopt:
http://www.adoption.com/

Epilogue

Now that our three adopted children are out of the nest, I can see that we walked a very thin line as we struggled to use our own faith and love to counteract the abuse and trauma of their earliest memories. I also know that walking this line takes a great deal of personal sensitivity to each child, along with a constant effort to understand where each one is coming from, every hour of every day. Brian and I discussed our children's needs daily. He had so much good common sense, and I had a wealth of experience with children as a teacher. If we had it to do all over again, would we still adopt them? Yes! What better thing could we do with our lives?

In hindsight, it is always easy to see where we might have done better. For instance, I wish we had sent Chris to a small private pre-school and elementary school. This would have fit his sensitive personality and need for attention and discipline. I believe his bright mind would have blossomed. It would also have freed Tommy from the watchful and critical eye of his brother. I thought they would look out for each other, but they didn't. When they were small it was hard to decide which needs were most important for the long term. Now I feel that a peaceful educational environment was what Chris needed, while Mary and Tommy needed the special help that only the public schools were equipped to give them.

Another thing I wish is that I had taken some classes on understanding teenagers. All of my training was for primary children. When our children entered the teen years, I was at a loss because my own teens were spent in a convent. Brian had a lot of trouble during this developmental stage, too. Having grown up as the youngest of a large family, he simply spent his teen years working to help support himself and his parents. What advice could he give to young teens who were playing computer games and had problems with ADHD? We all made it through, just as other parents do, with the help of understanding teachers, doctors, councilors, relatives, and neighbors. In many ways, raising adopted children is no different from raising your own biological children. They are all difficult to raise. That's part of being a parent, and we enjoyed and treasured all that we could.

We are glad that we adopted our three children. We are a family and always will be. It has been rewarding to be so needed and loved at the same time. We do hope that other people will see beyond the difficulties and be inspired to dedicate their lives as parents to children who so desperately need them.

Acknowledgments

I would like to thank all the wonderful members of the Longmont Writers Club who insisted that I not give up on this book, and who put in many hours of critical effort so it could be done well. I also wish to thank my friends in the Spirit of Peace parish for their support. Brian and I cannot thank our families enough for all they contributed to our family by their faith and values.

Author's Note

Although this story is an accurate history of our family's journey to wholeness, the names of all the people mentioned in these pages (including mine, as author) have been changed.